CALLED TO INTERCEDE

Volume One

DR. MONIQUE RODGERS

& AN ELITE COLLABORATION OF DYNAMIC
AUTHORS

FOREWORD BY DR. SHIRLEY CLARK

United States of America

Published by Shooting Stars Publishing House 2021

Copyright © 2021 Dr. Monique Rodgers

All Rights Reserved.

ISBN:9798776655111

This book has been published with all reasonable efforts taken to make the material error-free after the consent of the author. No part of this book shall be used, reproduced in any manner whatsoever without written permission from the author, except in the case of brief quotations embodied in critical articles and reviews.

The Author of this book is solely responsible and liable for its content including but not limited to the views, representations, descriptions, statements, information, opinions, and references. The Content of this book shall not constitute or be construed or deemed to reflect the opinion or expression of the Publisher or Editor. Neither the Publisher nor Editor endorse or approve the Content of this book or guarantee the reliability, accuracy or completeness of the Content published herein and do not make any representations or warranties of any kind, express or implied, including but not limited to the implied warranties of merchantability, fitness for a particular purpose. The Publisher and Editor shall not be liable whatsoever for any errors, omissions, whether such errors or omissions result from negligence, accident, or any other cause or claims for loss or damages of any kind, including without limitation, indirect or consequential loss or damage arising out of use, inability to use, or about the reliability, accuracy or sufficiency of the information contained in this book.

Dedication

This book is dedicated to intercessors that are on the frontline of prayer. Thank you for your continual sacrifice as a watchman on the wall in prayer for others.

Table of Contents

Foreword

Dr. Shirley K. Clark

Foreword

The sustainability of the church has always been contingent on prayer. As the Patriarchs and Matriarchs in the Bible prayed and built altars to seek God, there was always an outpouring of God's grace, favor, and anointing. Blind eyes were opened. The lame walked. Demonic spirits were expelled. Lives were changed. Increases and shifts were always a part of the equation. So, as we are a part of the 21st Century church and global prayer leaders, we are commanded in the Word of God to continue to keep prayer alive and aflame within our hearts.

While the Prayer Movement is not in its infancy any longer, the next generation of Apostolic and Prophetess Prayer Leaders must arise. Dr. Monique Rodgers is one of these that God is raising up to not only carry the mantle of prayer, but to lead a people into the presence of God.

As Nehemiah in the Bible was troubled by the gates and walls of Jerusalem being broken down, and needed repair, Dr. Rodgers, a model day Nehemiah, has also been troubled by God by the bleeding wounds of nations. The sound of their cry has provoked her to create this anthology, **"Called to Intercede."** This book is a timely tool as so many global intercessors have gotten off of their birthing stool. The Bible says men ought to always pray and not faint. Dr. Rodgers is being used by God to activate His intercessors *again* to lay hold of the altar, and to cry out for nations (Psalms 2:8). Every pastor, church leader, elder, minister, and intercessor, needs to read this book.

Every major move of God was birthed out of prayer (Upper Room, Azusa, etc.). And every person in the Bible who prayed, God moved on their behalf. Abraham prayed and a city was saved from destruction. Moses prayed and the Red Sea parted. Elijah prayed and the heavens were shut up for three and a half years. Joshua prayed and the sun and moon stood still. Esther prayed and God delivered a whole nation. Jehoshaphat prayed and God sent an ambush against his enemy. Hannah prayed and God gave her a son. Daniel prayed and God delivered him from the mouth of a lion. The disciples prayed and the floor shook. The church prayed and Peter was delivered from prison.

Paul and Silas prayed and that which had them bound fell off of them. And Jesus prayed and Elijah was raised from the dead. Whatever problems that are going on in our lives or in the nations, prayer will always be a part of the solution.

"Called To Intercede" is a clarion call for every believer. It is a prophetic declaration for the church to arise and to come to the city gates with their destroying weapons in their hands (Ezekiel 9:1).

I pray that this book will ignite a fire within you that will provoke you to fall on your knees NOW, and to cry out to a Holy God. "This is the confidence that we have in Him, that, if we ask anything according to His will, He heareth us" (I John 5:14).

Dr. Rodgers, thank you for this excellent resource tool, and I pray God's blessings over your life. Now, intercessors, let's open up our mouths and reshape history!

In His Love,

Dr. Shirley Clark

Founder/President, Shirley Clark International Ministries

Founder, Jabez Global Prayer Network

North Texas Regional Coordinator, National Day of Prayer

Served as National Prayer Coordinator for the Rosa Parks' "Protecting Freedom Campaign"

CEO, Clark's Consulting Firm, LLC

International Best-Selling Author

About the Intercessor

Prophetess Aida Eghill

Prophetess Aida Eghill carries years of experience and expertise as an intercessor and operates in the five-fold ministry gift. From the beginning years of the 80's until current she exudes an impeccable level of excellence to her Call of duty as an intercessor. Prophetess Aida Eghill is also a licensed Evangelist in 1998. She composed a training manual for intercessors in 2008. She established and founded Wheel of Prayer Ministry International while she resided in Florida. She is the current president of Covenant Prayer Partners Ministry International. She served as a volunteer prayer minister for Prayer and Crisis Referral Network. She also served at Destiny Worship Center International Church in 2006 and facilitated the intercessory ministry team. Prophetess Aida Eghill also served as an Evangelist and Administrative Assistant for Faith Deliverance Cathedral Church for two church locations in South Florida. Amongst other kingdom duties included she has also served as the coordinator for the Women's Conferences. She is an anointed prophetic worshiper and has written a playwright called, The Birth of Christ, a play that blessed many lives.

Prophetess Aida Eghill collaboratively works with Dr. Monique Rodgers, who is the visionary and Author of Called to Intercede International, as an Anthology Co-Author which is the Number One Best Selling Author on Amazon. She is Dr. Monique Rodgers personal administrator for Repairing the World Through the Word Ministry.

CHAPTER 1

Processing of the Intercessor

Our first and foremost purpose when serving in any capacity of ministry is to acknowledge that we were created in God's image and likeness to worship Him. Therefore, we must diligently seek after Him for a revelation of who we are and the "Ministry Call" that has been placed upon our lives. When we are submissive and obedient to God then He reveals this to us.

To be an effective intercessor we must know that God has called us with an assurance; despite our individual opinions, lineage, lack of education and/or knowledge of the "Call." We have been chosen and equipped for the work, but it needs to be cultivated through the planting, watering of the word of God and groomed by much prayer and fasting to subdue fleshly desires that will hinder and stagnant the growth to evolve into powerful prophets, intercessors, and warriors for God. Romans 12: 1-2 (KJV), "I beseech (urge) you therefore, brethren, by the mercies of God, that you present your bodies a living sacrifice, holy, acceptable to God, which is your reasonable service. And do not be conformed to this world, but be transformed by the renewing of your mind, that you may prove what is that good and acceptable and perfect will of God." As intercessors we must be willing to yield and sacrifice our body for labor and conduct warfare in the spirit which goes beyond the call of duty (our personal affairs and challenges); meaning when serving God wholeheartedly and singleness of mind there isn't any time restriction or restraints in performing ministry. 2 Timothy 2:4 "No man who warreth entangleth himself with the affairs of this life, that he may please him who hath chosen him to be a soldier."

When there is an urgency, mandate, clarion call given by the Holy Spirit we must be committed and willing to heed the "Call" despite inconvenience or sacrifice. As intercessors we must remember there is great accountability, a charge that has been assigned to us by God; when we do not pray, we delay or prohibit someone's breakthrough, life crisis, deliverance, etc. from being rescued. Intercessors are the front line of defense in the spirit realm. We are the firefighters, the officers of the law of God as we protect and serve our communities, regions, and nations.

The intercessors are on 24-hour Zone Watch in the earth, ready to respond at any time 365 days a year, 24 hours a day, 7 days a week. We are notified and contacted directly by the Chief and Commander, Jehovah Gibbor, the Lord Mighty in Battle and Holy Spirit that fuels us with the Fire of God, and our radar, covered by the Blood of Jesus and whole armor of God, we stand ten toes down ready to conduct spiritual warfare.

When there is a sound of disturbance, intrusion, war or breakout of cruelty and injustice in the land the Intercessors are the front line of defense, armed and dangerous taking territories, regions, dominion destroying the Satan's kingdom of darkness, evil kings and ruler and spoiling the spoiler to reset the order of God by any means necessary.

Intercessors are the firemen and firewomen; through the leading of the Holy Spirit, we mark targets to ignite the burning fire over geographical locations and city populations to burn out the spirits of infirmity, depravity, spiritual and physical suicide ideation. We release rivers of living water through the dry places as we decree and declare the word of God over territories. Intercessors are the law enforcers. We are the officers of God's law to protect and to serve our government, judicial systems, communities, counties, and cities by executing the written word of God over the wickedness in high places to demolish every stronghold.

The intercessors should be encouraged and know that Jesus is sitting at the right hand of God making intercession for us. We must remember that James 5:16 the effectual fervent (intense, hot, diligent) prayer of a righteous man avails much.

Evangelist Pauline Mendo

Ms. Pauline Mendo is the Founder & CEO PBM Enterprise, Inc., The Mendo Group LLC and Co-Founder of Write On LLC. Pauline is a fearless and faithful servant in the kingdom of God. She comes equipped, trained, and is anointed as an evangelist, preacher, teacher, missionary, and a deliverance minister. Pauline is an active member and an ordained and licensed Minister Evangelist at her current church home as a Servant Leader at Action Chapel Virginia, under the Leadership of the Presiding Dr. Bishop Kibby and First Lady Elsie Otoo. She is an Accountant and a student at the University of Maryland College Park, MD.

CHAPTER 2

Possessing the Mantle of Intercession

Every believer is called to be an intercessor because we are all called to prayer. In the book of Luke 18:1 "Then Jesus told them a parable about their need to always pray and not lose heart" another translation says Men ought always to pray! Prayer is for a Christian what water is for a fish in the sea. Prayer is something we cannot live without. It's like not having air to breathe, that is what prayer is for a believer. Prayer is a way of life; it is a lifestyle. If you plan to be a successful victorious Christian, you must pray. Muslims pray five times a day. They do not let anything interfere with their prayer time. A Muslim will stop whatever they are doing and pray whenever it is time for prayer! Orthodox Jews pray three times a day morning, noon, and night. How many times a day do you pray? Will you make prayer a priority? Will you submit to the call of an intercessor? Will you give yourself to prayer just a little longer than the average person! Will you wait to hear from the heart of God the Father? If the answer is yes, then you are ready to possess the mantle of an intercessor!!

What is prayer? According to Google "Prayer in the Bible is how believers of God talk to him; it is how they made their praise and requests known. The Scriptures are filled with beautiful examples of people crying out to God and asking for his strength, guidance, healing and more.

Prayer is our way of communicating with God. It is God's way of communicating back to us. According to Philippian 4:6, "Be careful about nothing; but in everything by prayer and supplication with thanksgiving let your requests be made known unto God." Prayer not only becomes a lifestyle but also becomes who you are!

To possess the mantle of prayer we must first define intercession. According to the Merriam-Webster dictionary online, intercession is, "1: the act of interceding 2: prayer, petition, or entreaty in favor of another." It says the act of interceding, my God! It is something you must put in action! It is who you are the moment a person petitions a need, or you pick up that something is going on with them you immediately go into prayer for the person or their family. It is instantaneous, it does not take a thought! It is not an inconvenience because you know it is for the wellbeing of others, it is your pleasure, and it comes easy for you to pray, my God! You are graced to pray and stand in the gap on behalf of someone you don't even know. You are working as a co-labor with God on behalf of the King of Kings! According to Wikipedia.org another definition for intercession or intercessory prayer is, "the act of praying to a deity or to a saint in heaven on behalf of oneself or others,"

An Intercessor is defined as: a person who intercedes. It is an honor to be called an intercessor as you are called upon by God to be a mediator for someone that has an immediate need! You are now co-laboring with God for the service in the kingdom of God. 1 Corinthians 3:9 (NIV) says, "For we are co-workers in God's service; you are God's field, God's building." As we are called as intercessors, we are doing the work to empower God's people everyday people whether strangers, someone's son, or someone's daughter you just never knew at the time. God may have you to just pray without giving you the details because he is entrusting you to be ready and available at any given moment to stand in the gap and be a mediator for someone or something that is very important which may be a matter of life and death! I will be honest there were times I failed to pray immediately when I was prompted to pray and realized that something was wrong, a distance and it was the Holy Spirit.

You have answered the call to make intercession your priority. It is a mandate that God has placed on you to answer on behalf of someone you may never meet. God is using you to change lives, to change destinies, to move mountains to help save nations on behalf of God and for the advancement of His Kingdom!

You must be devoted to prayer for the mantle to be possessed! You must be someone who gets engulfed in prayer. I can recall in my early walk with God I was attending a church in Silver Spring called Bethel Senior Pastor Johnson was the leader and they had all night prayers on Friday nights. I remember feeling excited about tarrying and interceding with the intercessors. It was electrifying. I felt like the heavens were opened. Later as the night progressed, the more intense the prayers were. I remember feeling a little tired and even falling asleep during the third watch of the night which is between midnight and 3 am. I was tired and I woke up to the intercessors praying loudly with great intensity, so I jumped up and began to pray till 6:00 am. Our prayer leader who had never stopped praying came over to me and said you need to come back again and pray until you are able to stand. Your flesh must die. I came back the following Friday night for evening prayer service. This time when we prayed, he prayed over all so that we would not fall asleep but travail in prayer. He released the mantle of intercession. It was like fire! I stayed up praying until 5:00 am nonstop. It was like something hit my spirit and I never felt tired. I kept praying with the team I believe at that time I received the mantle to become an intercessor. It was at that service I heard from the Lord, and he said would you pray another hour! I recall in Matthew 28:36-41, Jesus was in Gethsemane about to surrender to his death! He desperately needed intercession to submit to the gruesome task ahead. It was heart wrenching, and he needed the disciples to intercede on his behalf that he would fulfill the task! As an intercessor you are needed especially in times of great distress and where clarity is needed the hand of God must be demonstrated. Jesus needs the disciples to stay awake and make intercession for him. The scriptures say. Then Jesus went with his disciples to a place called Gethsemane, and he said to them, "Sit here while I go over there and pray. 37 He took Peter and the two sons of Zebedee along with him, and he began to be sorrowful and troubled. 38 Then he said to them, my soul is overwhelmed with sorrow to the point of death. Stay here and keep watch with me.39 Going a little farther, he fell with his face to the ground and prayed, My Father, if it is possible, may this cup be taken from me. Yet not as I will, but as you will.40 Then he returned to his disciples and found them sleeping. Couldn't you men keep watch with me for one hour? he asked Peter. 41 Watch and pray so that you will not fall into temptation. The spirit is willing, but the flesh is weak," (Matthew 28-36-41).

The disciples fell asleep like I did when I first started out, but I did not give up. The spirit is willing, but our flesh is weak, and it takes practice. It takes the activation of the power of the Holy Spirit to take over. Praying in tongues is essential; it is what ignites the intercessor in you to pray God's perfect will for the matter. Praying in the spirit is God's perfect will being put into flourishing. In the book of Romans 8:26,

"Likewise, the Spirit helps us in our weakness. For we do not know what to pray for as we ought, but the Spirit himself intercedes for us with groanings too deep for words." Praying in the spirit is powerful. It speaks the mysteries of the spirit of God that otherwise would not be known. We have access to God's expressed thoughts towards humanity. We have the upper hand. We can destroy the works of the devil and enforce the will of God on earth. We can rest assured that the will of God will take place! As I said before, I kept praying on my own and eventually when I was assembled with other intercessors prayer was birthed out of me. I want to encourage you never to give up. Keep praying. The moment you wake up at 3:00 am or 4:00 am, know that the Holy Spirit is waking you up to get up and pray. You do not need to know the details, just pray. Once I understood that prayer is a lifeline for the believer and the unbeliever I never stop praying ever again!

MANTLES ARE CAUGHT NOT TAUGHT, as you can see the relationship between Elisha and Elijah in 2 Kings 2:13 (KJV)

'He took up also the mantle of Elijah that fell from him, and went back, and stood by the bank of Jordan." In the Berean bible translation 2 King 2:12-14, "As Elisha watched, he cried out, "My father, my father, the chariots and horsemen of Israel!" And he saw Elijah no more. So, taking hold of his own clothes, he tore them in two. 13Elisha also picked up the cloak that had fallen from Elijah, and he went back and stood on the bank of the Jordan. 14T Then he took the cloak of Elijah that had fallen from him and struck the waters. "Where now is the LORD, the God of Elijah?" he asked. And when he had struck the waters, they parted to the right and to the left, and Elisha crossed over."

Elisha caught the mantle and went to work as some of you are going to catch the mantle from your prayer closet, from your leaders, from your prayer captain when I came up it was church mothers who were the church intercessors over the prayer ministry in the church it was the grandmothers that were the chief intercessor prayer captain that took on the different prayers watch. When you possess the mantle of the intercessor it not a chore but who you are God has graced you to pray for hours and it may seem like you have only prayed an hour, but you can get lost in prayer when you begin to pray in the spirit it ignites a fire on the inside of you! You might say what is a mantle? If you take on the mantle of something, such as a profession or an important job, you take on the responsibilities and duties which must be fulfilled by anyone who has this profession or position. Possessing the mantle of an intercessor is a great responsibility, it can be life or death! You are in a profession for the kingdom of God that is essential. It is the heartbeat of the ministry and is necessary for the local and the global body of Christ to function. You are the most important part of the five-fold development of the ministry. The intercessor is the pulse of the heart of God.

WOW! What an honor to be chosen as a believer, to be called to be an intercessor. You have now possessed the mantle of the intercessor as you stay in a posture of prayer. You have partnered with God the Father to advance the work of his kingdom. Will you answer the call to intercede? Are you ready to possess the mantle of intercession?

About the Intercessor

Dr. Monique Rodgers

Dr. Monique Rodgers is an ordained prophet, visionary, intercessor, international best-selling author, CEO, motivational speaker, entrepreneur, educator, and literary genius. Dr. Rodgers excels today as a notable writing coach, founder, and serial entrepreneur.

Throughout the course of her career, she has written such prolific works such as, Hello! My name is Millennial, Picking up the Pieces, The Majestical Land of Twinville, Falling in Love with Jesus, Accelerate, Overcoming Writer's Block, Just Breathe, and Called to Intercede Volumes 1-4. She has also been included as a co-author in collaborations such as, Jumpstart Your Mind, Speak Up We Deserve to Be Heard, Finding Joy in the Journey Volume 2, and Let the Kingdompreneurs Speak. Due to her outstanding breadth of experience, Dr. Rodgers has been featured on Rachel Speaks radio program, The Love Walk Podcast, The Glory Network, God's Glory Radio Show, The Miracle Zone, The Healing Zone. She also graced several platforms worldwide. She served as a TV host for WATCTV. She has been featured in Heart and Soul Magazine, My Story the Magazine, Kish Magazine's Top 20 National Authors of 2021. Marquis Who's Who in America 2021-2022. She also assisted in various volunteer work including an executive team member for Lady Deliverer's Arise, Aniyah Space and she also a board member for I am my sister organization. She is also a certified master business coach, certified vegan life coach, and health advocate. She has served on various leadership positions in business and in ministry. She is currently a prayer hub leader for the city of Raleigh under the tutelage of Apostle Jennifer LeClaire. She is also a team member of CBK where she serves in ministry for Sofia Ruffin. As an expert in her field Dr. Rodgers earned her undergraduate degree through Oral Roberts University as well as a Master of Science degree and a doctorate in global leadership through Colorado Technical University. She has also studied at the Black Business School online as well as Harvard University Business Online. Looking towards the future, Dr. Rodgers intends to expand upon her expertise and continue serving through ministry for God. She aspires to help over one hundred authors to complete and publish their books and help intercessors to draw closer to God.

CHAPTER 3

The Intercessor God's Hidden Agent

When you think about a secret agent what comes to mind? You may visualize a detective with a magnifying glass in hand searching for answers. But an intercessor is so much greater than a detective as they are the expert secret agent that covers others through prayer and intercession. They are also the secret weapon that God uses as a conduit of his continual strategic instructions given on earth. Intercessors share the heart of God and pray for others continually. Intercessors represent the heartbeat of prayer and its intrinsic expectations for others who are in daily need. The intercessor becomes the direct line of access to Heaven as they pray and bombard the courts of Heaven on behalf of others. As a secret agent intercessor, you serve as a prayer line and a lifeline connection. The lifeline connection point is where the intercession operates as a lifeguard on behalf of those who are the recipients of prayers that are waiting to be answered. As the hidden agent, there are mysteries and revelations that God downpours, conceals, and reveals to the intercessor to begin to immediately pray for individuals that need urgent intervention through the courts of prayer.

Hidden agents have a connection as well as an access point that is not often seen and recognized by others. This is imperative in that as a hidden agent there are disclosures that are given from God to the intercessor that is serving as the hidden agent to carry out the exceptions and deliberations that are being given through prayer. The magnifying glass in the spirit realm is used to show the intercessor what needs to be covered, the word of God the decoder is used to cover and protect through God's word. Jeremiah 33:3 (NKJV) says, "Call unto me and I will answer you and show you great and mighty things in which you do not know." God wants to speak to his intercessors that are listening to the hidden mysteries that are disclosed in prayer and intercession. There is such a multiplicity to prayer as intercessors hold the hidden keys to unlocking on behalf of others.

As secret agents, the identities of intercessors may never be known or even heard of as their role is one that is not easy in the world. There are a series of sleepless nights and countless moments of intense warfare on behalf of others. The sleepless nights are graced with compassion in knowing that the prayers are not in vain. Each hidden agent intercessor understands the assignment of intercession as being one that is indeed a mandate that serves to honor God through praying and intervening on behalf of others. It is an opportunity that serves as one that is selfless but not helpless. The intercessor is given supernatural strength. Each hidden detective intercessor is given their own secret identity to battle and war on behalf of others within the spirit of prayer. Many intercessors do not recognize their calling until later in life but some like me recognize it early on and can train and prepare for the battles that arise. Just like the detective is an investigator, God will use us at times to pray in the Holy Ghost and pray the mysteries of Heaven on behalf of those who do not have the strength to pray because they are worn and torn from the turbulence of life. God wants to provide clarity, strength, and endurance to every intercessor that has been encountering tough times in their families, jobs, ministries, and in their personal times of prayer. May you now receive the strength that only the Holy Spirit can give you to continue this journey and in this race as God's undercover agents.

About the Intercessor

Aleshia Brown

Aleshia Brown is a wife and mother of four children. She is a graduate of James Madison University. She attends Grace Cathedral Ministries and is under the covering of Apostle Sammy C. Smith. She has accomplished many feats, such as self-publishing a Series titled Diary of a Single Mom, writing an anthology collaboration with other authors titled "From the Pit of Pain to the Paradigm of Purpose." She has written an article for an international magazine in New Zealand titled "Her Story." The Overseer of Empower Me Global Ministries and works alongside her husband as the CFO of The Carla Rose Foundation. She is a kingdom metamorphosis writing coach that elevates, equips, and empowers women to be bold, beautiful, and branded in their purpose and kingdom assignments through writing. Her writing course Writing 2 Destiny was designed to empower and educate women on the importance of writing and equip women to write their way to destiny.

CHAPTER 4

The Effectual Fervent Prayer of the Righteous Avails Much

You may have heard this verse quoted many times and from many versions, "Confess your faults one to another, and pray one for another, that ye may be healed. The effectual fervent prayer of a righteous man availeth much," (James 5:16). That last part of that verse is what I came to understand in a time of physical testing. Effectual is defined as, "capable of producing an intended effect," (https://www.dictionary.com/browse/effectual) Effectual prayer is a prayer that hits the target. The word fervent speaks to having or showing intensity of spirit (https://www.dictionary.com/browse/fervent), Both terms manifested themselves in healing taking place in my life through the effectual and fervent prayer of my own child.

My mouth was closed, and I could not utter any words. The pain was excruciating as I felt the pressure in my brain as if someone was squishing my brain while hammering it with a steel hammer. It affected the rest of my body. I could barely walk, nor could I sit up. It felt like my joints and muscles were being tied into knots. I felt helpless. The pain prevented me from speaking. All I could say was Jesus please take this cup from me. Jesus, ease the pressure. As I lay there in tears, God felt my tears flowing and heard the helplessness in my voice.

My daughter came in and asked "Mommy, can I pray for you?" She began praying a prayer of thanksgiving because she already believed and agreed with God that I was healed. She said, "Father in the name of Jesus, I thank you for making my mommy feel better. I thank you for healing my mommy. I thank you for giving my mommy strength. I thank you for covering

and protecting my mommy under your wings. I thank you for the blood covering my mommy. In Jesus Name, Amen." She then began chanting, calling on her forces. She chanted, "Holy Ghost power activate, Holy Ghost power, activate, Holy Ghost power, activate, activate, so my mommy can be strong." She said this repeatedly and would not stop until she saw the results. As she spoke these words of victory into the atmosphere, I could feel the pressure lifting off my brain. I sat up in the bed and could feel the pressure lifting even more.

"Out of the mouths of children and infants You have ordained strength, because of your enemies, that you may silence the enemy and the avenger," (Psalm 8:2). "He called a little child to him and placed the child among them. And he said: "Truly I tell you, unless you change and become like little children, you will never enter the kingdom of heaven. Therefore, whoever takes the lowly position of this child is the greatest in the kingdom of heaven," (Matthew 18:2-4).

Dr. Vinita Johnson

Dr. Vinita Johnson is a Pastor, Author and Entrepreneur. She is a retired United States Army Warrant Officer of 21 years of active-duty service. She is the author of "Autopsy of a Dead Leader" and founder of the Women's Empowerment Center to inspire, motivate and encourage others to achieve their dreams. Her mandate is to build, equip and send out well able ministers to empower and impact their community in a positive way.

CHAPTER 5

The Power of Pressing

What will come out of you when the squeeze is on? Matthew 14:32-34 says, "They went to a place called Gethsemane, and Jesus said to his disciples, "Sit here while I pray." He took Peter, James, and John along with him, and he began to be deeply distressed and troubled. "My soul is overwhelmed with sorrow to the point of death," he said to them. "Stay here and keep watch." According to Easton's Bible Dictionary, Gethsemane means oil-press. It was a place of pressure, where Jesus expressed anguish to what was ahead. When life presses you into a difficult space and you see no way out, press in as if it's life or death. Don't retreat or fall back into the hands of the enemy, for he desires to destroy and devour you. Satan is the author of confusion that uses plots and ploys to distract and deter those from seeking God's will for their life. 1 Peter 5:8 says, "Be alert and of sober mind. Your enemy the devil prowls around like a roaring lion looking for someone to devour." Therefore, press into the will of God that would leave a mark that can't be erased.

Heavenly Father, I give you all the glory and praise for you are worthy to be exalted in all the earth. Through every test, trial, and distress you continue to answer every prayer and deliver me from the hand of the enemy. Your strength is greater than any pressure and adversity that I will ever face in life. Father, you are faithful and just to never allow me to experience more temptation than I could bear with a way of escape. I thank you that my mind shall be renewed and transformed by every discerned test that comes to waver, frustrate, and diminish my faith. I shall press, not give in or up by standing firm in the midst of the enemy's voice and wicked attempts to destroy my peace and joy. For you are my great strength and strong tower, protector and defender that hides me in the cleft of the rock. There shall be no troubles or perplexities from any side that shall cause me to walk in despair or distress. Every tear that flows from the anguish and affliction of my heart shall be washed by your love, grace and mercy that endures forever. Amen!

When you are faced with adversity and it seems as if God is not present or near, call on the name of Jesus and experience His everlasting love and provision. In the book of 1 John 5:14 says, "This is the confidence we have in approaching God: that if we ask anything according to his will, he hears us." Continuously confessing the promises of God teaches your mouth to speak life and not death, which trains your heart to trust and believe the true rhema Word. Begin speaking what God says and see your life align with his established plans and promises that have been predestined.

Father, thank you for hearing my cries during my pain, sorrow, and disappointments in life. I have absolute confidence that you will provide for my needs even in my worst moments. I shall stand fast and unmovable through my inability to see beyond my natural sight. I am focused and driven by your strength to prevail in victory. Thank you for establishing my footsteps by leading and guiding me into places of favor with You and man. Amen!

The pressures of life can wear you down to a point where you want to give up. Your strength comes from the power of God, who is your rock, fortress, and deliverer. God is well able to bring you through tests and trials that challenge your faith even in times of brokenness. Pressure exposes your inner man and the depth of your faith in God. James 1:3-4 (The Message) says, "You know that under pressure, your faith-life is forced into the open and shows its true colors. Let it do its work, so you become mature and well-developed, not deficient in any way." Pressing through adversity brings strength and resilience that testifies to the power of God that works in your life. God is developing and preparing you to endure in times of hardship; intercede and minister to those in need as you walk in your purpose for His glory.

Father may your mighty works mature and develop me in every area of my life. Leave no lack or deficiency as I carry out your plan on the earth. Shape and mold me into the ambassador you desire for me to be with boldness, power, and authority. When the squeeze is on, I can be confident that the battle is already won. For the enemy has been rendered inoperative, non-effect, and void against your created vessel. Satan has no power or dominion over me, my family, marriage, children, ministry, or finances. I trust you at your Word and shall not look left or right, but only unto you as my Lord and Savior. In Jesus' name, Amen!

As you travel this journey and press toward the goal to win the eternal prize, do not look back but ahead to Jesus Christ, the author, and finisher of your faith. Shalom!

Dr. Katrina Esau

Dr. Katrina Esau is the founder of W.H.O.L.E. (Wives Healing Openly Leaving Him Exalted) ™ and the creator of The W.H.O.L.E. Academy, which offers programming that cultivates healing and forgiveness. Her ministry was birthed after coming face to face with infidelity in her own marriage, having bouts of hopelessness, and feeling alone in her marital journey. Her mission in life is to help other women hurting from the pain of infidelity reclaim their power and walk in total healing. Dr. Esau is known for her unique style of delivery and coaching that has a way of reaching people where they are and empowering them to come up higher.

Dr. Esau is the author of The Pain of Infidelity Births Purpose where she shares her story and experience with other women in a real, raw, and relatable way to bring hope, encouragement, and healing to them whether they are entering in, in the midst of, or they walked away from a season of trauma in their marriage. She is also the author of The Blueprint to Becoming Whole, which is the accompanying journal with activities, affirmations, and encouragement.

Website: www.drkatrinaesau.com

CHAPTER 6

A Divine Gap Stander

Intercession is a tool given to us by God. To stand in the gap for others is a privilege and an honor. Standing for others is one thing, it's quite another when you are standing in the gap for your spouse, your child, or your bloodline. In 2003, standing in the gap took on new meaning to me. Infidelity hit my home and my husband was not ready to do the work. I was hurt, angry, embarrassed, ashamed, filled with guilt, rejected, abandoned, you name it. I didn't want to fight. I wanted out. But God had a different plan. His plan was to prosper me and bring me to an expected end. That meant restoration, healing, and. deliverance. I had been chosen to stand in the gap for my husband's deliverance, it was divine.

God used my spiritual mother to guide me according to His principles. She showed me how to lean on God. Despite what I saw, to trust God. Her words to me were, "You will stand in the gap." She didn't ask me. She made a declaration. I thought to myself, "Excuse me? Why do I have to stand in the gap? He doesn't want to fight for our marriage." I just wanted to be free and stop hurting. I didn't understand the need to stand in the gap when the desire wasn't reciprocal. It was through this trial I truly learned the power of standing in the gap for others. Oftentimes people don't know how to pray for themselves. They don't know how to fight. If we've been given the gift of intercession, it is important for us to use it. My husband's desires or his ability to stand was none of my business. It was up to me to walk in the gift of prophetic intercession to see not only my husband's life transformed, but my marriage, and my bloodline. Divorce was a generational curse, and it was time for it to be broken. While I thought it takes two to make it work, I quickly learned the second person didn't have to be my husband. It's easy to fall back on Matthew 19:9, which says adultery grants approval for divorce and I did try that, but when you're in communion with God and the Holy Ghost, He'll also remind you of other scriptures. Like Matthew 19:8 that says the bill of divorce was only given because of the hardness of your heart. Or Isaiah 59:15-16 where God was displeased because there was no one to intercede on behalf of the truth. How about Ezekiel 22:30 when He searched for a man to stand in the gap for the sake of the land that He wouldn't destroy it. You get the gist.

Sometimes the two have to be you and God. Since I'm a three-part being, my flesh was stuck in the hurt and trauma. I went back to God saying, "The word says where two come touching and agreeing on anything, it shall be." At the time, my husband wasn't in agreement. So, I asked God, what do you want me to do? He responded, "Come in agreement with me and my word." I didn't quite understand the depth of what that meant. Yes, I knew what it meant to come into agreement, but we use that term in the natural sense—two human beings in the physical. He was taking my level of trust and intercession higher. It is not always possible to have a person agree with you, but we can always come in agreement with God and His word. One thing is for sure and two for certain, His word will NEVER fail or return to him void. Okay, God, I'll stand in the gap. My prayer changed to asking God to place forgiveness in me heart toward my husband. To use me as a tool of reconciliation for my marriage (be careful what you ask for). I learned to use the scriptures to decree and declare the word of God over my husband, my marriage, myself, and my child. The promises of God are YES and Amen! His word can NOT return unto Him void.

There is Power in Standing in the Gap on Divine Assignment – Being a Divine Gap Stander What started looking like it would be a short separation shifted. God instructed me to tell my husband he had three days to come home. Three days turned into three years. As you can imagine, I felt a little like Noah as days, then years passed, and there was no movement (so it seemed). BUT GOD! He's faithful to perform His word. After three years, my husband finally decided to come back home. The decision was great, but it was only the beginning. Now, God had to put Him in isolation to get to his heart. Off to prison, he went. So much more happened in these next three years, but the moral is standing in the gap led to healing, restoration, a book (The Pain of Infidelity Births Purpose), a journal (The Blueprint to Becoming Whole), an academy that is centered around healing and forgiveness that helps women walk through the hurt and reclaim their power, coaching clients, speaking assignments, and so much more. My marriage is better now than it was before the infidelity. Will you seek Him? Will you stand in the gap as He divinely orders?

I AM A DIVINE GAP STANDER

About the Intercessor

Rochelle Baker

Rochelle Baker is a Kingdom Entrepreneur, Psalmist, intercessor, published author and CEO of Rochelle Baker Publishing. She Is a powerful woman of God who has been called to intercede and prophesy for the kingdom of God. Her Mission Is Build Up And

Equip the Kingdom while building generational wealth and legacy.

CHAPTER 7

The Power of Generational Prayers

Did you know that as a Kingdom Citizen we have the power to pray for Generations? Our God is an eternal and an everlasting God. His Existence has no end. He cannot be measured or limited by time or space because he is Alpha and Omega, The Beginning, and the End; he is the first and the last. His very being and who he is will forever exist from generation to generation. Secondly, we serve a covenant keeping God (Genesis 9:12). When God makes a promise to us as his children, his word must do exactly what he sent it out on the earth to do. It cannot return unto him void or fall to the ground! (Isaiah 55:11) If God says you will be blessed, then you will be blessed. He is not a man. He cannot lie.

We have so many examples of generational prayers/promises God has bestowed upon us. I would like to draw your attention to (Genesis 17:7). In this text, God confirmed the Everlasting Covenant with Abraham and his descendants for generation and generations to come. Being seeds of Abraham that means we're included in this covenant yay!!!!

Which also means we can remind God of his promise towards us however, not only for ourselves but also for our generations to come. Through Christ Jesus, we have the power to plead our case and command the blessings of God through prayer by speaking, commanding, decreeing, and declaring God Words and promises out of our mouths now and for future generations.

My first real memory of prayer was when I was a little girl. I was about 9 or 10. My grandmother would make me, and my four siblings gather in a circle with her and hold hands as she prayed every morning before we went out the door to school! Now that I am older and wiser, I know that she was praying a prayer of protection. It is funny to me now because she would pray the same prayer so much that I had it memorized and planted down in my soul. I remember joking with my siblings mocking her prayer. I had no idea how powerful her prayers were. I now understand that my grandmother was an intercessor. As an intercessor, myself, I have been trying so hard to remember her prayer.

Here is what I remember.

Father God here it is again in thy presence and in thy Sight. We come again to thank you, Father God, for all the many blessings that you have bestowed upon us. Lord, we thank you for waking us up this morning in our right minds and starting us on our way. Lord we thank for the food on the table, Clothes on our back, roof over our heads and so much more. We thank you for leading and guiding us from day to day. She would then press in and pray for the sick, shut in, homeless, abuse, neglected, and rejected. At the end, I remember her praying for us that no hurt, harm, or danger would cross our path to and from school!

My Grandmother prayed always. I know in my heart that her and my lineage of children and grandchildren are still living off her prayers. As I compare my family to those of others around me although every family has their own generational curses on the bloodline (that we have the power to break thank you, Lord!) I can say we have truly been blessed. Blessed with ridiculous favor and grace. We have not had any deaths nor premature deaths in decades in fact the last funeral I remember going to was hers in 2012. All the children and grandchildren are healthy. No mental illness of birth defects. We all have always had more than enough. We have always had a roof over our heads, never been homeless. We never lacked anything. Favor follows me everywhere I go, and people tell me all the time you got favor on your life. Without her life of prayer and faith, I would not have the foundation of God rooted in me from childhood. I was truly trained up in the word of God and I have not departed from it. I might have backslid a few times, but God's word never left my heart.

I've always had the heart to pray for others. If I saw a need in someone's life, I would pray that God fills that need and he would. However, it was not until I began to see the physical manifestation of my prayers being answered. It has increased my faith in the power of prayer and has been my testimony as to why I encourage others to pray. I know as God continues to answer my request surely; he would do it for you and your generations.

Join me in prayer as a pray for our generations to come:

Father God, right now, I decree and declare the blessing of the Lord (Deuteronomy 28:1-14) and ridiculous favor, long life, good health, and prosperity over our lineage now in the name of Jesus. I pray that the blessings of the Lord will overtake them. I declare Malachi 3:10 over them: Lord may your fire surround them and be a hedge of protection over them making them unmovable, unshakeable, and impenetrable in the physical and spiritual realms. I lose Angels to protect them from any hurt, harm, or danger all the days of their lives. May the Ancient Word that you spoke over their lives come forth and manifest unto the earth as you have written with no burden added to it. May the blessings of the Lord pursue and overtake them in due season. I renounce any spoken or unspoken word curses I have spoken over my bloodline, in Jesus' name. I come out of all agreements and covenants giving the enemy legal access to my bloodline, now in the name of Jesus. I seal this prayer with the blood of Jesus. Amen, Amen and Amen!

About the Intercessor

Wynika Williams

Wynika "Queen" Williams is a Kingdom ambassador, emerging leader in ministry and marketplace, wife, mother, author, serial-entrepreneur, scribe, mentor, activist, poet, and podcaster.

CHAPTER 8

The Heart of An Intercessor

Intercession is standing in the gap for others in the posture of prayer with love and compassion; it is the heart of God and His language. Just think of it! Jesus and the Holy Spirit are interceding for us and they want to use us as a tool to intercede for others. But, to be an effective intercessor, we must crucify attitudes, prejudices, and personal grudges, to exchange our hearts for God's heart.

Ezekiel 11:19-20 NKJV

Then I will give them **one heart,** and I will put a new spirit within them, and take the stony heart out of their flesh, and give them a heart of flesh, that they may walk in My statutes and keep My judgments and do them; and they shall be my people, and I will be their God.

Testimony…

One Sunday morning I was on the app called Clubhouse in a room titled Intercession *and Prophetic Flow.* The intercessor began praying in the room and immediately picked me up in the spirit. I had been suffering in silence with depression for quite some time and I was desperately begging God to heal me. After she prayed, they invited me to go up to the stage to get personal prayer. During that time, God revealed to the intercessor all the pains, heartbreak, and hardship that I had endured. God also showed her my bruised and broken heart, something that I didn't even know that I had been operating with until that moment. That morning, God performed supernatural heart surgery on me, and I received a new heart. A heart that was full of His love, mercy, compassion, and made of flesh.

Effective intercession requires one heart, not two.

As intercessors, it's vitally important to allow God to not only mend our broken hearts but replace them with His heart. Before I received a supernatural heart transplant,

I found it very difficult to intercede for others because I was praying from a wounded place instead of a healed and whole place. I was like the intercessor/prophet Jonah in the bible. Jonah was an Old Testament prophet, who God sent to Nineveh to declare His judgement on the city for its wickedness so that the people would turn from their wicked ways and repent, but Jonah fled and went to Tarshish. Jonah had hatred in his heart for the city's wickedness and refused to put his pride and hatred to the side to intercede on their behalf.

As intercessor's it's our job to intercede for others to turn their hearts back to God, but we can't intercede properly if our heart posture is out of alignment with the will of God as an intercessor. We must lay aside every sin and every weight that so easily ensnares us. It is only in the place of vulnerability that God can give us one heart, the merging and blending of our heart with His as two hearts become one. We can't get caught up in our personal feelings of pain, opinions, agendas, traumas, and feelings and allow that to be a stumbling block to our intercession for others. With hearts of flesh, we will feel what God feels and His heart feels pain. It pains God to see His children in such a broken and fallen state. Ask God to give you a heart that will obey His instructions, a yielded heart that will stand in the gap and intercede for our families, cities, nations, and a fallen world.

God's heart is the standard within His Kingdom, and everything He does reflects His heart. As intercessors, our hearts should always be willing and available for God's use; a heart that is locked away is unusable. God wants to give you His heart for the nations. Will you allow God to use you as a tool to intercede for His people?

Prayer for an Intercessor's Heart

Father in the name of Jesus Christ of Nazareth. I humbly come before your throne, worshiping you in spirit and in truth, acknowledging how great, mighty, and sovereign you are. I enter your gates with thanksgiving and into your courts with praise. Father, I repent for the omission and commission of my sins. I am thankful for your forgiveness and that you remember my sins no more. I ask that you create in me a clean heart and renew a right spirit within me (Psalm 51:10). Father, you are the great cardiologist in the spirit. Do surgery on my heart and break off every hard area of my heart. According to Ezekiel 11:19, give me **one** heart and put a new spirit within me, take out my heart of stone and give me a heart of flesh. A heart that will obey, a heart that loves and a heart that will intercede and stand in the gap for your people. Thank you, Father, for performing supernatural heart surgery and giving me a heart of flesh. I declare that my new heart overflows with the love of God. I bind up every assignment from the enemy that would try to make me put up barriers over my heart that would cause me to be unavailable to God. I declare that my new heart will allow Jesus and the Holy Spirit to make intercession through me. I declare I will allow God to be my rear guard and I will make my heart available to God at all times. I plead the blood of Jesus over every part of my new heart, and I allow God's love to flow through me. I seal this prayer with the power and the precious blood of Jesus. Amen!

About the Intercessor

Lydia Rose

Lydia Rose is a grief recovery coach with over 20 years' experience facilitating grief recovery in private, group and workshop settings. She served as a Missionary, Hospice Chaplain, Youth Leader, and Intercessory Prayer leader. Lydia spends time nurturing, guiding, and building Young Women to find confidence in God and themselves to process the everyday issues that feel overwhelming. Lydia is known to be compassionate, motivating, and encouraging.

Her recent project as host of Grief Talk w/ Lydia provides a safe space for the broken-hearted to talk through their grief while receiving life supporting tools and techniques to navigate through their season of grief. Lydia tells her story through an eBook about her process through grief when her mother transitioned suddenly in August 1999 the day before their family reunion. Joy in your Mourning became a reality when her heart was put to the test.

Lydia also found strength in journaling, so she penned her journal, *Pray, Journal and Heal* as a guide to help heal from broken places in their life that is available on Amazon.

CHAPTER 9

The Tender Heart of An Intercessor

The heart of an intercessor is tender before God. The heart of an intercessor aims to please our God. My heart belongs to Jesus. It is Jesus whom I yearn to please. I cry out to him in ways that I cannot reach out to any other. He hears my cry daily! As it says in His word, "If I call upon him and pray to him, he will listen to me."

My tears are liquid prayers, and he wipes them away with his comforting peace. God is mindful of my tears. (2Timothy 1:4) When I seek him with all my whole heart, there is peace during a storm. There is peace amid sorrow. When I cry out from the quiet places of my heart, I will find him. (Jeremiah 29:12-13) An intercessor with a surrendered heart brings joy to God, so daily I say, "Create in me a clean heart O God and renew a right spirit within me." The cleansing power of the blood of Jesus keeps us in right standing with God. The power of the blood Jesus consumes everything that is not like God. God made us to be His righteous intercessors by surrendering our hearts to Him to be cleansed. Then we will receive the instructions on how to intercede for others and ourselves.

What is an intercessor? What is prayer

An intercessor is someone who prays on behalf of another, according to Wikipedia. An intercessor will plead, weep, petition, urge, counsel, and war against the enemy, just to name a few functions of the role. Intercessors talk to God concerning those who at one point cannot do it for themselves, or we might touch and agree with them. Intercessors guard the heart of those who need prayer to preach the Gospel. I am called and chosen by God, handpicked, some have said. Often, I wonder why? I wonder why I was chosen before the foundation of the world to be right here speaking to you as you ask the same question. The Father said, "Come forth, Lydia! You are fearfully and wonderfully made (Psalm 139:14,) and I have put greatness within you. I have put My word in you. I have given you the unction to intercede on the behalf of others. Now is the time!" This is such a humbling position to be in. God made my heart tender to serve as an intercessor. Sacrifice shapes the surrendered heart of an intercessor, hurts, pain, rejection, and trials that pull you closer and closer to God's heart. An intercessor's heart has the burden of God. I say what He says. I must live to breathe his breath of life daily as I go to Him in prayer on behalf of others. As an intercessor, my life has changed tremendously, because it has taken my focus off of just me and on to others. I feel the weight of God's Glory when I take time to pray for others to receive their healing, deliverance, strength, or peace. Intercessors can bring a solution or an answer to a problem. We are partnering with Jesus, our great Intercessor! What an honor!

The Difference between Prayer & Intercession

Prayer is having a "one-on-one" with God. He talks to me, and He listens to me. He embraces my cares with His love and gives guidance. The Lord orders my footsteps. He said that I am free to ask of him and he will answer (Psalm 4:3); but know that the Lord has set apart him that is godly for Himself. The Lord will hear when I call unto Him! I am so grateful that the Lord hears my cry. He listens to the cry of my heart. Scripture says before I call, He answers (Isaiah 65:24.) He already knows what I need and when I need it. But I must first ask and believe that I will receive what I stand in the need of. Matthew 21:22 says, "And all things whatsoever ye shall ask in prayer, believing you shall receive." I have learned that prayer is essential to live this life. Prayer is my lifeline. I couldn't imagine not talking to God daily. I need Him in every way to guide me. He is my decision maker. He is my healer. He is my great deliverer, and this has all been revealed through prayer. Prayer will transform us. Prayer will keep us humble and cause us to place God above everything and everyone. The heart of an intercessor realizes that without God, we are nothing!

In conclusion, remember these few things to strengthen your heart as an intercessor:

- Wash your heart & hands daily in the spirit of repentance (Psalm 51)

- Obey God (Acts 5:29)

- Let God's desires be your desires (Psalm 37:4)

- Discern the voice of God

- Pray the scriptures

- Love, Love, Love as you serve and Intercede

About the Intercessor

Willette M. Hurst

Willette M. Hurst is a highly sought-after international speaker, life coach, the Founder of Driven 2 Empower U, LLC, and a mother of two, and grandmother. A prolific writer, Willette has authored and published 3 books titled, *Don't Kill Your Vision For Another Man's Baby, Do It Now! Tomorrow Is Not Promised,* and *Over Due: Inspirational Stories That Will Push You To Birth Your Dreams, NOW!* Her books are a testimony and truly inspirational account of her life and are a must-have for someone who needs that extra motivation to believe in themselves again.

Born in Santa Monica, California, and raised in West Hollywood, Willette had a normal life - a home and a good job until she fell sick at work in 2012, and her life changed completely. When the doctor declared that she was irreversibly disabled, things changed suddenly, and everything she had spiraled out of hand. She lost her job, was evicted from her home, filed for bankruptcy, and spent nearly six years living from her car and people's homes from California through Georgia. Even worse than losing what she owned, her self-worth, self-esteem, and self-respect plunged.

After moving to Georgia, Willette spent the next 3 years trying to collect and rediscover herself. Rather than feel a victim of the events that had occurred in her life, she found in them her purpose to inspire and uplift others. Instead of bitterness, she found healing and restoration. She learned to love the person she was and began to focus on utilizing what she had gained in the loss for her own benefit and that of others.

Having found her calling and started the journey into ministry amidst her homelessness, Willette has showcased incredible persistence and dedication to reinstating other people's shattered dreams and helping them to discover their authentic selves. Through Driven 2 Empower U, LLC, Willette has impacted hundreds of lives, helping people, young and old alike, overcome their tough experiences and derive value from them as building blocks to a better life.

For the past 10 years that she has been an evangelist, Willette has had a profound and remarkably fulfilling experience. She has evangelized to people at every platform God has given her, preaching a message of hope from retail stores, gas stations, and international conferences, and workshops. She has established herself as an astoundingly supportive mentor, empowering people to reach their dreams and visions and explore the immense power God has put in them.

Willette's life is an affirmation that, with determination, no challenge cannot be overcome and, most importantly, a mirror that reflects God's grace on those who believe in him.

CHAPTER 10

Warring Outside Of The Four Walls

The entire Christian life is a battlefield. We are born for battle, and the scripture makes it glaring (Eph. 6:12). One of the truest shreds of evidence that a believer is growing is his or her ability to acknowledge and embrace the reality of warfare. However, the Bible establishes that the weapons of our warfare are not carnal but are mighty through God to the pulling down of strongholds (2Cor. 10:4). We are in warfare, but our enemies are invisible. We are in a more terrible battle than physical combat. Spiritual battle is the deadliest form of warfare, and it is inevitable.

The focus of this chapter is warfare outside of the four walls. It is the most productive of all kinds of strategies for spiritual battles. Although its potency is in the spirit, it produces physical results, as it generates tremendous power against the enemy. Warring outside the four walls is to intercede, make petitions, or request in favor of another. It is to contend for one's highest good in every situation until manifestation happens.

One problem that believers have, which has resulted in the increased rate of evil occurrences in the world, is our failure to intercede for others and our dear nation. Most believers are not selfless in their prayers. All they think of is their family and their job. What happens outside their family seems not to concern them. We should remember that whatever affects our environment will either have a direct or indirect influence on us. More so, intercession is a responsibility that saddles every believer. 1Timothy 2:1-2 says: "I exhort therefore, that, first of all, supplications, prayers, intercessions, and giving of thanks, be made for all men; For kings, and for all that are in authority; that we may lead a quiet and peaceable life in all godliness and honesty."

The number of burdens you bear for others can measure your spiritual maturity. Self-centered prayers are not as weighty as those that accommodate the needs of other people and the nation. You become a change agent when you think beyond your family to see a need in our world, in our society, or in the lives of people that are not even related to you biologically, and you still care to take it to God in prayers. Jesus intercedes for Peter in Luke 22:31-32, and the survival of Peter was equal to the rising of several others. What if Jesus didn't intercede for him? What if Christ was self-centered? It will interest you to know that Jesus intercedes for all believers in John 17. Even before you came to God, Jesus had contended for your soul.

Several depressed, hopeless, and poverty-stricken people are walking around in our streets. They need us to intercede for them. It's high time we war outside the four walls of our comfort zones. This is the hour to bear the burdens of others in the place of prayers. Our government has taken enough criticism at various levels, but it is time we engaged in prayers for them. Those citizens of our nation acting wrongly are doing so under the influence of spiritual forces that have taken them captive. But we can break demonic strongholds and prison gates in the place of intercession. We can set the captives of darkness free when we present the matters of our erring nation to the Lord. God is looking for intercessors that will supplicate for the territories they found themselves in. He wants to save sinners based on our request and intercessions on their behalf.

God lamented because there was no intercessor in Ezekiel 22:30-31 where He said: "And I sought for a man among them, that should make up the hedge, and stand in the gap before me for the land, that I should not destroy it: but I found none. Therefore, have I poured out mine indignation upon them; I have consumed them with the fire of my wrath: their own way have I recompensed upon their heads, saith the Lord GOD." God would have had mercy on our dear nation if He found intercessors that will plead for her. Our government wouldn't have made decisions that are indecent to her citizens if we had interceded for her. We direly need intercessors like Abraham, who bargained so much with God over two cities- Sodom and Gomorrah (Gen. 18:17-33). Although Abraham had no child, he didn't put his personal needs first; rather, he took the burden of Sodom and Gomorrah upon himself.

We need intercessors like Moses, who would rather have his name blotted out of the book of life than to have the whole Israelite perish in the wilderness (Ex. 32:11).

Instead of accepting God's promise to raise a nation through him, Moses pleaded with God on behalf of the rebellious Israelites. That sinner in your street can get saved if you will intercede on his behalf. Likewise, the church of God and the entire world can experience another mighty move of God if we put on our spiritual armor and get to the battlefield on our knees. Charles Spurgeon said that prayer moves the hand that moves the world. And I believe such prayers are not self-centered.

Regardless of the pains that Stephen went through when he was being stoned to death, he said: "Father, forgive them" (Acts 7:60). That was such a strong plea for mercy on behalf of his persecutors. Instead of condemning them, he interceded for them. It is not out of point to trace the conversation of Saul of Tarsus to such an act of supplication. Intercession is a great spiritual weapon capable of transforming any seemingly, impossible situation. The force of intercession is like bringing God to a dialogue table over the matter of an individual or nation. And there, God agrees to your terms. I liken it to the wrestling of Jacob with an angel (Gen. 32:24-25).

There's no record in the Bible where intercession was unfruitful. And it won't happen in our day either. Isn't it surprising that an angel descended into prison and brought Peter out when the church interceded for him (Acts 12:5-7)? How pathetic is it that James lost his head because the church didn't pray (Acts 12:2)? When the church remains silent and selfish in prayers, we have indirectly allowed the devil to do as it pleases him. But when we rise to the responsibility of intercession, we will save ourselves and the coming generation from the hands of the wicked. Can your knees be bent in the place of prayers for others, the body of Christ, or the world at large? Will you be the intercessor God is looking for?

About the intercessor

Natasha Bibbins

Natasha Bibbins, is an Evangelist, Prophetess, Co-Author, Author, Assistant Pastor and Jurisdictional Liaison for Zion Community Churches of Hampton Road in Virginia. Natasha Bibbins Ministries consists of Forever Fire Empower, LLC and Sisters Empowering Sisters Ministries. She learned the importance of prayer and intercession during her 5 years of minister-in-training. She realized that she was a seer prophet and was anointed before being ordained in 2019.

Natasha also became a Best-Selling Co-Author in 2020 for the Dreamer on the Rise Book, compiled by Dr. Kishma George. Natasha believes that knowledge and wisdom is the key to being effective in any ministry.

Professionally, Natasha has a master's degree in Management, a bachelor's degree in Business Management, and an associate degree in Business Administration. While working on her bachelor's degree, she also received a certificate in Bible Studies from Christian Leaders Institute. Currently, she is a Doctoral candidate at Regent University.

Natasha is married to Michael Bibbins, and together they have six young adults and a granddaughter.

Natasha's favorite scripture is Romans 8:18: *"For I reckon that the sufferings of this present time are not worthy to be compared to the glory which shall be revealed in us."* Amen.

CHAPTER 11

I am an Intercessor!

The Assignment:

So many times, in my life I could not understand why I was always being asked to pray for someone. I recall moments of feeling like I needed someone to pray for me, but somehow, I would always end up praying for others. It was not until I heard the term "intercession" that I was feeling this is who I am. Although I felt like this is who I was, I still didn't quite understand the duty of an intercessor. When I was younger, I would hear the mothers in the church say, "you will understand it better by and by." Well, by and by, I was understanding the start of my assignment as an intercessor. I grew up in the country where the ONLY thing we could do was to go to church, and it seemed as if we were there seven days a week. If we were not in school, we were at church. When you are a child, your purpose is not clear, so it is hard to understand what the will of God is concerning you. One thing that speaks true is that you may not understand your assignment, but when your foundation is set, you have no other choice than to build on it.

First NFL Game:

I took my husband to his first NFL team game. I was there only to enjoy the game, and for no other reason. As I was sitting there, I could clearly see what the Lord was saying to me about being a true intercessor. I told my husband that the Lord was speaking to me.

At this game, the Lord was giving me a visual of what my prayers should do. This is what the Lord showed me. There is a team that is working hard to get to their promise, (goal line), but there is always something there to interrupt them from reaching their promise. Here, it is the other team. As they are going down the field, the quarterback is trying to connect with his players on his team, but there's just one problem, the other team is trying to steal the promise.

As you create this visual, it is you that's on the team that is fighting to get to your promise. Every time your opponent tries to knock you down, it's your intercessor standing right there to intercede on your behalf. Because your opponent is fighting you, they are not paying close attention to know that your helper was nearby. The intercessor is the best blocker that money could never buy. Can you just see how this is playing out in your mind? Can you see what it means to help others reach their promise? Therefore, every intercessor must have the Holy Ghost because they to be led by God when to step in and snatch what should have broken the intended person down. Keeping in line with what God showed me, when you stand in the gap, there is that chance that you might receive exactly what was meant for the person who you were praying for. You must be ready to fight and at all costs. Do not stop praying because of the possibility, but rather keep praying because of the purpose. If God is using you to pray for someone, there is always a reason. Please, don't stop praying.

Praying for Change:

It was during a time in my life when it seemed like God didn't hear my prayer because He wasn't answering them. I was questioning my calling to be an intercessor, or did I just enjoy praying. I am questioning my purpose. My phone rings from someone asking for me to pray for their marriage. The human response wanted to say, "I'm going through my own marital issues. I can't pray for you!" If we are honest, that is exactly what we do, but being an intercessor, you can't! I know you are reading this and might say "why not?" I will tell you, as one that is called to pray for others, you understand that you speak the heart of God. Ask yourself, do you think that Jesus would ever stop interceding on your behalf? No, for the Bible tells me that Jesus is sitting on the right hand of God, making intercessions for us. If Jesus makes intercessions for us, what makes those called to intercede to stop making intercessions for others?

It can't happen. God would ever turn His back on your prayers. If we speak the heart of God, that means we take on His heart as well. By the spirit of God that's in us, we always intervene without question. Romans 8:26-27 says, "And the Holy Spirit helps us in our weakness. For example, we don't know what God wants us to pray for. But the Holy Spirit prays for us with groanings that cannot be expressed in words. 27And the Father who knows all hearts knows what the Spirit is saying, for the Spirit pleads for us believers in harmony with God's own will."

When An Intercessor Prays

I hear many SAYING that they have been called to be intercessors but have a strong opinion about what they are praying about. The truth is that as Intercessors, we have strong discernment and have a strong sense of knowing what prayers should go forth and what prayers should be given to God for Him to have His way. A prayer that goes against the Word of God is a prayer that has been given to God for Him to take control because as an Intercessor, your opinion does not matter. To intercede means that you pray and intervene on the behalf of others. In other words, you give up your right to judge the prayer. This is when the gift of the Holy Ghost becomes prevalent in our prayers. The Hebrew word for intercession is "paga," which means to "meet." As intercessors, we are finding ourselves in a meeting with God all the time. One might think, what do you mean when you say we have a meeting with God? Well, it's simple. Let us look at this in the natural, when we come together in an office setting to discuss a particular subject, called a meeting. Whether it's a two-person meeting or ten, it's still a meeting. As intercessors, we create that same environment, a meeting with God. When you pray, you are praying for something to happen. We expect change. This is what makes an intercessor separate from a person that loves to pray. Pray with expectation. Pray for a shift. Pray for results.

Prayer

Father, please give us a better understanding of the calling of intercessions. We need more understanding of the knowledge passed down to us throughout the years. Father, make clear what we need and weed out what we don't need. We are available and willing to pray until something happens for others. Thank you, Lord, for calling us to be your intercessors on the wall. In Jesus Name, Amen!

About the Intercessor

Jessica A.A. Highsmith

JESSICA AA HIGHSMITH is a life-long resident of North Carolina. She enjoys time well spent with her husband, and sons. Called by God, a prophetess and seer, she enjoys ministering to others and helping people to see themselves as God sees them. She's keen on building individuals to be Kingdom citizens to develop their own personal relation with God through healing, deliverance and faith especially concerning those called to entrepreneurship and or the corporate sector. She's a book publisher, author of several books, screen scriptwriter, psalmist, serial entrepreneur and Christian life coach. She's been featured on radio shows, university campuses, churches, magazines, social media interviews and foster care advocacy summits. She has always served as an advocate for the voiceless or the Misfit in areas such as: Prayer Strategies to Navigate Corporate Careers, Foster Care and Adoption, Mental Health, Resilience Coaching, Radical Faith. Resilient Wives and STEAM – Science, Technology, Engineering, Art, and Math.

For booking or more information: www.EmpowerMeEnterprises.com

CHAPTER 12

Strategic Navigations

Prayer Strategies for Navigating the Corporate Sector

Father, in the mighty name of Jesus, I come to you seeking your direction and your guidance and wisdom necessary for me to perform every work, every skill that you have placed specifically within me according to Exodus 35:35. You have given me a sphere of influence that I am to care for (Genesis 2:15). When interacting with colleagues or those that you have put under my charge, allow me to use your wisdom in communication with them (Job 31:13).

God, I ask that as it pertains to financial affairs in marketplace ministry, in business or entrepreneurship that I receive fair wages as you have ordained according to the work and skill of my hands. I declare I will uphold integrity when operating with laborers and contractors and those contracted to complete work (James 5:4).

God, don't let me be one who oppresses those that are below me for my gain (Proverbs 22:16). Let me be the lender and not the borrower in business affairs so that I might be a kingdom financial steward and distribution center (Psalms 112:5.). Lead me in conducting negotiations, contracts and deals in godly integrity and wisdom (Deuteronomy 25:13). God, let me be humble enough to use the wisdom and skills you have given me and the skills of the people you have tasked to work for me or alongside me. Allow me to experience iron sharpening iron (I Peter 4:10-11).

Let me not despise the days of my small beginnings. God, let me work while I have time to work and let me gather, the knowledge, the emotional stability, and the wisdom needed as you maximize my capacity to get wealth (Proverbs 13:11) so I won't to be foolish because of having gained in a hurry and having a lack of wisdom, knowledge, and understanding which will lead me to poverty (Proverbs 14: 23).

Let me remember to tithe and bless you with what you have been so gracious to bless me with (Proverbs 15:16). God let me be one who walks in integrity from the ground up of building (Proverbs 28: 6). Cause me to honor workplace leaders the way as in your word (Proverbs 27:18). God, send people to my business that come with a servant's heart (Matthew 20:26).

Grant me the resilience to be diligent with the work of my hands, so there is no lack in my household (Proverbs 10:4; Proverbs 12:24). God, don't let me be sluggish, don't let me be tired, don't let depression and anxiety oppress me and keep me in a dark place. Lord, keep me out of the pit. Lord, protect my workers and my colleagues from falling into the cave and pits of tiredness, feeling of being rundown and burnout as according to Proverbs 13:4, Proverbs 19:15, Proverbs 20:4. Proverbs 22:13 and Proverbs 21: 5.

Grace me to be the person who will complete work that is needed. Allow people to connect to me that are change agents that will see what needs to be done and look for ways to improve a system, a process, a place, a thing as according to the vision you have given for that business, and that whatever their hands might find to do God allow us to have the knowledge, the thought to do it (Ecclesiastes 9:10). Allow me to not get weary in laying the groundwork that must go forth in building a business. God, help me understand that the person who is faithful over little, you will make them ruler over much (Luke 16:10). Protect me from leeches that will come and desire payment without toil. Lord, block these demonic assignments in the name of Jesus (II Thessalonians 3:10-11). God, teach me and my team how to work to gain your kingdom and wealth because you said, "the wealth of the sinner is laid up for the just, * (Proverbs 13:22). Lord, I pray you give us discernment, wisdom, and understanding that we know how to use our knowledge according to what you have imparted to us with your Holy Spirit to gain wealth without having to toil and kill ourselves. God let us work smarter and not harder, according to Proverbs 23:4.

God, strengthen my hands, my body, my mind so that I won't run away in fear from the thing you may use to bless me in the sector within my business, as according to Nehemiah 6:9. God, allow me to always remember assignment over profit according to Mark 8:36 and let me remember it is your grace that I can carry out these things and not my strength. Let me remember that the Holy Spirit is with me and therefore I can endure and outlast some of my counterparts, some other businesses not because of my strength but because of the Grace that you have given (I Corinthians 15:10).

God, order my thoughts and my steps. Give me understanding of the time and the seasons of when to do things. God, establish everything that I have committed to you. You know the plans of my heart for my future, my business, and my career. God, cause me to seek godly advisors, wisdom, and kingdom counsel from those that have gone before me or who can give insight. God, any plan that I have that doesn't align with your will, I give you free rein to close every door.

God, I stand on the biblical principles that are outlined in Proverbs 15:22, Proverbs 15:15, Proverbs 16:9, Proverbs 6:3, I Chronicle 12:32, Proverbs 19:21, and finally Proverbs 20:18, In Jesus' name, Amen.

About the Intercessor

Rhonda Fraser

Rhonda P. Fraser is a global women's leader who considers her Christian Faith paramount. She has been married to Rev. Reginald Fraser since 1988 and together they have three beautiful children. She is an empowerment specialist, inspirational speaker, personal development/leadership coach and functions in women's leadership/advisory roles for several organizations, including churches, mostly in New York. She co-authored six books and is a bestselling author for the following inspirational books: 1) *Resilient Faith: Dare to Believe* (Lead Author and Compiler)2) *Women of War: Peace in the Midst of Storm* (Co-Author) and 3) *This is How I Fight My Battles* (Co-Author). Her 2021/22 new release book is *Empowered to Overcome Tough Seasons of Life*

Rhonda is an accomplished corporate finance, marketing, and strategy expert, with a Master's degree (MBA) from Villanova University. She has been featured on FOX, CBS, and NBC news and on various billboards.

Website: www.rfraserconsulting.com
Facebook: Rhonda P. Fraser
Instagram: @rhondapfraser

CHAPTER 13

The Call of the Cross and the Crown

The cross of Jesus represents a perfect picture of God's love for the world. It shows two important components of life relating to the divine call upon our lives: the vertical call between God and man, and the horizontal call among humanity. This foundational aspect of our purpose is so important that Jesus summarizes the ten commandments with the two essentials: loving God and loving our neighbor as ourselves.

Communing with God through prayer and through intercession (standing in the gap for others) helps us to fulfill the divine call. God's desire to commune with man is clear from the beginning, when He came down daily for that time together. His call "Adam, where are you?" shows His desire for connection, which led Him to summon another call in Heaven, asking, who will go to bridge the gap of the broken communication with man? The answer to His call was "I will go, send me" by the great intercessor himself, His Son, Jesus, granting man access back to God.

Intercession is so important that Jesus made it a priority while on earth and He is still making intercession for us. At a critical juncture of His life on earth, when he was on the way to the cross, He asked His friends to watch and pray with Him, but they fell asleep. So many of us can relate to either falling asleep on others or experiencing others sleep on us when support was necessary. Jesus' piercing response to His friends was, can't you watch with me for one hour? The question is still being asked today. Can we intercede for others in their hard season? Are we able to stand in the gap and help them bear their burdens/crosses? Can we extend the love to our neighbors as we would want for ourselves?

Communing with God helps us to have the correct approach to life's journey. Failing to answer the call to watch and pray made the disciples unprepared to face the valley season of Jesus' journey, resulting in their carnal response. When we are not intentional in heeding the call to intercede, our response, particularly to the hard seasons of life, is often inappropriate.

Everyone will have some challenging situation–some "cross" to bear, but when God's people call on Him, His supernatural power shows, help, and peace come, lives transform, promises received and purpose fulfilled! Heaven is ready to respond to our call when done consistently in obedience, faith, sincerity, humility, and alignment with God's plan. Here are a few examples of these miracles.

Our call to God protects us from danger. Daniel called on God three times a day and God answered–the lions' mouths shut. Engaging heaven silences fearful situations. Our call to God brings fire from heaven, like Elijah experienced, while his opposers toiled all day, calling their gods to no avail. God's power is matchless. Our call to God brings freedom. Peter experienced a miraculous release from prison as believers interceded for him. Intercession breaks bondages. Our call to God gives guidance. Before venturing out to battle, David asked God, "should we pursue?" God's direction prevents us from fighting unnecessary battles.

Our call to God brings confidence that His plan is still on track, even with detours in the journey. Joseph experienced unfair twists and turns in life, but in the end, he stood in the gap to save his family and confidently declared, "you meant it for evil but God meant it for good."

Our call to God brings alignment with His plan. Hannah's prayers aligned with God's purpose when she stood in the gap to offer her son as God's prophet, by uttering, "if you give me., I will give back ..." That alignment released her miracle. We get Jesus' attention, like blind Bartimaeus did, when we push forward and ignore discouragement or anything that tries to silence our call to the Lord.

The thief on the cross witnessed the miraculous power of that call when He declared "Lord, remember me when you come into your Kingdom." Jesus responded immediately with, "TODAY, you will be with me in paradise." A simple, sincere call from earth got heaven's immediate response and instantly changed that man's destiny from darkness to light. His call moved him from his cross of damnation to a crown of everlasting life. Jesus is still answering those emergency calls for miracles and changing destinies from hopelessness to eternal hope. All it takes is a sincere "Lord, Remember Me!"

So many of us can testify how God remembered us after we called on Him or after someone interceded for us. We have seen divine healing, provision, favor–salvation! Many times, we feel a burden to intercede for people who are facing battles we are facing or have faced. I have shared stories in the various books that I have written about how God performed miracles for our family and others when we called on Him. One significant miracle is when God overturned the doctor's report that my husband and I would never have biological children. God blessed us with three beautiful children.

Now we intercede for people facing the same situation and have seen answered prayers -many times beautiful babies birthed, sometimes just about nine months after interceding for them. However, the call to intercede expands beyond the cry, Lord, remember me, or Lord remember us and grant relief from the crosses we bear from time to time in life.

The call extends to eternity where we intercede for souls, so that the crosses we bear and the cares of life do not overwhelm us and cause us to lose the eternal crown of life that the Lord has promised to those who love Him, as mentioned in Revelation 3:11. Yes, the ultimate call to heaven is that we overcome the cross and get our crown, like Jesus did.

About the Intercessor

Joyce K. Adams

Joyce K. Adams is God's chosen daughter. She is a proud mother of 3 amazing children and a grandmother.

Joyce has encountered fear, rejection, and doubt throughout her life. She found her purpose through her past. Her purpose is to help other people by exposing the lies that are holding them back and empower them to walk in their Uniqueness.

CHAPTER 14

It's Not Too late

"Call to Me, and I will answer you, and show you great and mighty things, which you do not know." Jeremiah 33:3

Let me take you on a short encouraging journey. I thought it was too late. I was a Senior in high school when I found out that I was pregnant. I dropped out of school before graduation. A year after giving birth to my son, I signed up for night school to earn my GED, but I could not stay focused. I allowed self-doubt and fear to overtake my mind. I would hear, "You are stupid, and you will always fail." So, I dropped out of school not just one time, but 3 times. The thought of me going to school stayed in my spirit, but I kept hearing the voices, so I put it at the bottom of the box and tossed it in the attic, thinking it would never be found again.

Fast forward, I had a good friend I had known for years, and we decided to become a couple. I began to find myself idolizing him (soul ties). I would put his needs before God. There was a brokenness that I thought I could fix in him. We started having problems and decided to be friends, which broke my heart. In August 2015, I got a phone call Monday morning that changed my life. My friend died in a motorcycle accident. I dropped to the floor in anguish, for it felt like a big part of me had died. I could not believe it. I had just spoken with him not even an hour before the accident. I was mad at God for taking him away from me, hoping that He would bring him back to life. I found myself drinking wine and crying every day for a year straight. I suffered in silence.

When you think no one is watching, someone invited me to Church. They picked me up that Sunday, and as I walked into the sanctuary, tears rolled down my face. I found myself at the altar not only that Sunday but every Sunday afterward. I realized that I needed GOD so that I would not be stuck in my pain anymore. Suddenly God began to speak to me and tell me that I AM HIS CHOSEN Daughter. I felt like

Bartimaeus from the bible in the book of Mark 10:51-52 "What do you want me to do for you?" Jesus asked him. The blind man said, "Rabbi, I want to see." "Go," said Jesus, "your faith has healed you." Immediately he received his sight and followed Jesus along the road. God heard my cries, and He began to send people to help me. Before I knew it, it was 2018, and that task of finishing High School came back to my spirit at the age of 44. God had brought it back to the surface during my healing process.

I started High School in January of 2018; it was the 3rd quarter. Fear met me at the door, but I couldn't let it stop me this time. I knew this time was different from the challenges I faced before. Knowing and believing I would finish strong this time, my mind was set. With the help of the Holy Spirit, I was able to complete 4 classes with 3 A's and 1 B. After the Summer break, there were 4 classes left to complete. Everything was going well with school until tragedy hit my family in February 2019. My 22-month-old nephew was killed, and my brother and his baby mother needed me. I missed almost 2 months of school. However, my teacher (an angel) made sure that I had everything I needed to graduate, and that was all God. She retired right after graduation.

The enemy thought he was going to have me drop out of school a fourth time due to the death of my nephew. Now I need you to lean in. It is almost time for graduation, and I learned from the Adult Education High School that they do not allow you to wear caps and gowns to receive your Diploma. I was a little upset by that news, and I said, "Lord, You know my heart's desire." A day later, I received an email stating that they would allow all Adult Education students to wear caps and gowns from that year forward. Glory be to God. This accomplishment meant a lot to me, and I wanted the full graduation experience. I was the first child to graduate from my parents' offspring, and I completed the task with honors, not just from man but from God.

If you do not get anything else from what I have written, please remember that God used the tragedy to open my eyes and get out of a comfortable position. Romans 8:28 says, "And we know that in all things God works for the good of those who love him, who have been called according to his purpose." When God has given you an assignment that makes you feel unequipped, you must quickly seek God for help and TRUST HIM even when it does not look like it can be done. Time to decree and declare that "I can, and I will!"

About the Intercessor

Lauren Evans

Lauren Evans has completed a Bachelor's in Sociology, a Master's in Behavior and Rehabilitation Counseling, a Master's in Marriage and Family Counseling, and is currently completing a Doctorate in Business Administration. She is the author for the children's book {The Cat Called Tiger} and loves serving, giving, and helping people in need. She is a gifted poet and mime dancer.

CHAPTER 15

What is Prayer

Prayer is a conversation and understanding who God is to you is the key. You may have been surrounded by so many locked doors in your life because you saw the problems. You saw the hurts that family and friends were enduring. You were trying to hold everyone and even yourself together until your arms were too short of reaching it all. You had the key all along and didn't know how to use it. I am telling you this from someone who understands your pain. I understand your struggle and the frustrations that you can't always formulate. Have you ever gotten into a place to pray, and in the midst of it, your mind begins to wonder? I had that problem all the time when I first started getting my life right with God. I would listen to people around me say these magnificent prayers and ask myself, am I far from God? God would always whisper gently to me that the steps of a good man are ordered by the Lord.

He would sometimes then encourage me to trust my process. I am coming to you as someone who hasn't arrived at all in this thing. I am pressing my way through. Prayer once felt like a chore for me, but now it is something that I think about doing when I wake up in the middle of the night and can't sleep. A friend of mine introduced me to a resource called (Clubhouse). If you are someone new to prayer, they have a lot of great prayer rooms that start at various times throughout the entire day. This prayer resource guidebook is intended to meet you where you are and help you grow into the best version of yourself. I want to encourage you from my experience to ask God to help you sharpen your own identity, as he shapes your character daily. Prayer is a tool that can unlock so many doors. Can you imagine going to work and not knowing how to run the program? Can you imagine a mechanic preparing to work on your car without any tools? Prayer helps us to activate the power of the Holy Spirit. The Holy Spirit is a comforter that the Lord left as a reminder that we aren't alone.

The greater that lives on the inside of us is anxiously waiting for us to tap in. Can you imagine having a key to a car, needing to go somewhere, and never turning on the vehicle? The Holy Spirit is like the kid on the bleacher yelling (Put me in coach, I'm ready). The question isn't are you ready to grow in your walk with the Lord. Instead, it is "are you ready to receive the power to help you become the better you?" I would often be amazed going to church and watching so many people just weeping easily from saying the name Jesus. I was never that person. My natural father taught us to always be strong and never cry in public. God took me through a long process of learning how to do the thing that I was lacking. I needed to learn how to surrender. I experienced church hurt, false judgments, and slander by people I thought should have been praying for me. I am here to tell you; God resurrected that pain that I wanted to bury so that I can be healed. Sometimes you may go through things in life that will make you want to drift away from God.

When my mom passed away, I was immediately admitted into a suicidal facility the day of her funeral. I didn't know how to live beyond that pain. However, in solitude, God gave poems to help ease my pain. The pain didn't leave because I wanted to. I tried to pray, but I was mad and couldn't pinpoint my frustrations. Oh, but God! God took me through a journey that helped me to expound upon my identity in him. I felt led to partner in this project for those who are maybe experiencing rejection, loneliness, pain, and even the loss of a loved one. I can tell you that my heavenly father re-introduced himself to me and taught me a new way. A new way to mourn, to love, and to live. I started asking myself what kind of legacy I wanted to leave behind.

Many of these questions that the Lord dropped in my spirit actually began to help me reposition my position. Sometimes we just need to change our posture. We can examine stories in the Bible like Daniel and the Lion's Den. I would often ask myself, what kind of character did Daniel possess to obtain so much favor from the Lord? Another question that hit me hard when growing in my walk was, what made God pick the 12 disciples that he did? If God judges my lifestyle today on earth, would He pick me to be one of the 12? These tough questions made me want to learn how to love God. How do I use the keys in my hand to take me to the next destination? The only way to know these answers is to ask the one who created the clay. God formed us, knowing every single hair on our forehead.

You may not have all the answers today on how to get to that place that your heart envisions you to be with God. I want to encourage you to do something that may be very hard. Let Him drive. Let him take the wheel. Let him lead and guide you in the way that you should go. Take a moment and tell yourself, today I will lean not unto my own understanding. I will acknowledge him and let him direct my path. A baby has to learn how to put one foot in front of the other before walking. No person has the same journey. People may have similar stories, but no one's walk is the same. This is why prayer must become part of your daily language. Learning a new language in a different country can be hard sometimes. But it's easier to learn it in a country that primarily speaks it than one that doesn't. Prayer is the same way. Surround yourself with people who pray and make time to put yourself in an inviting atmosphere to the father. You have now been given another opportunity to use the keys He has given you.

About the Intercessor

Brandon VanHorn

Brandon VanHorn is the Presiding Overseer of Unity Faith Fellowship and Founder/Senior Leader of Brandon VanHorn Ministries. For many years he has served the Baptist & COGIC (Church of God in Christ) denomination and churches, while under the leadership of great leaders. Through continuous roles and servanthood Brandon has helped plant, start, grow, and build organizations and multiple churches. As of 2012 Brandon was affirmed as Prophet and found himself walking into the prophetic and apostolic mantle and calling as he partnered with non-denominational churches. His vision is to bridge the gap from generation to generation through connecting and networking with other like-minded leaders in ministry and marketplace by not trying to remain bound by the barriers of tradition, religion, and denominations.

CHAPTER 16

Are You Power Plugged?

Our source of power is the Holy Spirit and the Word of God. We build ourselves up in faith when we confess the Word. We experience greater confidence when we understand the Word and walk in revelation. Prayer and intercession plug us into the power source, which is God, allowing His power to flow to us in any situation. There are many types of prayer. Prayers of confession, praise, petition, spiritual warfare, and thanksgiving are just a few examples. The most apparent form of prayer that God seems to be bringing to the forefront in the current movement is indeed intercession. Intercessory prayer is quite simple. It is someone asking God to do something in a person's life, in the Church, or in a specific situation. It is coming to God on behalf of someone else. It is, in some ways, the most selfless, giving sort of prayer. It is ultimately one of the greatest acts of love.

A good picture of intercession in Scripture is the parable that Jesus tells of the friend who came at midnight (Luke 11:5-8). A friend had been on a long trip, and he came to his friend's house at midnight. The traveler is very hungry, but his friend has no bread to give him. The host goes next door and begins to shout and pound at the door for his neighbor to get up and give him some bread. The worst imaginable thing happens. His next-door neighbor doesn't even come to the door but just shouts out from his bed something like this: "Go away! I am in bed, and my children are in bed. Go away and come back in the morning!" Instead of giving up, the man keeps on pounding and shouting until his next-door neighbor gets up, grumbling and gives him the bread that he needs to feed his hungry friend.

Now I know Jesus tells that parable to teach us the power of persistence in prayer, to pray and never give up. But I want to suggest that this parable is also a perfect picture of intercession. I had preached a sermon on this, and I called it: "The Friend in the Middle." There are three friends. One has a need; he is hungry. Another friend can meet that need…he has the bread. And then there is the friend in the middle who brings the two together. He goes to one on behalf of the other, and this is where God has placed us in prayer. We are surrounded by a needy world. Everyone has spiritual needs, emotional needs, physical needs… and much more. We cannot fulfill these needs in others on our own, but we know the God who can meet and exceed them. We are called to go to Father on behalf of those around us in prayer.

Intercession is a powerful ministry and calling to pray for others. It is a tremendous blessing to see God work in others and their lives. God is calling the Body of Christ and the Church today to a whole new level of intercession. We see God do amazing things around the world because we are learning to intercede for the lost. We are learning to intercede for the world as a whole. God has shown us that prayer is the frontline strategy for reaching the unreached, breaking down barriers to presenting the Gospel, and planting His churches and building His Kingdom. It is astonishing what God is doing as we obediently pray His will into the lives of others. Understand that intercession is the closest thing we can do that emulates the current ministry of Jesus. Intercessory prayer is what Jesus is doing today: "because He always lives to intercede for them" (Hebrews 7:25). It is astonishing to realize that Jesus is praying for us as we pray for others.

There are a lot of things that Jesus used to do, such as build houses and catch fish. He died on a cross to save mankind. In like manner, He calls us from different professions to all participate in intercession. It is a powerful weapon for believers who have a hatred for the works of darkness (Ps 139:21). Do you want to see changes in your community, region, and nation? This is your right and inheritance as a son and daughter of the King. "As you pray, your pray, your Father will give you the world for an inheritance" (Ps 2:8). You have the power to change territories, regions, people, and outcomes of situations. When you reverence the Lord, you will hate evil, and your righteous prayers will reflect it. "The fear of the Lord is to hate evil: Pride and arrogance, and the evil way, and the forward mouth, do I hate. – Proverbs 8:13"

About the Intercessor

Apostle Genise Rodgers

Apostle Genise Rodgers is the founder of Fresh Wind Empowerment Ministry under the tutelage of Apostle Wayne Rodgers. She is the mother of our visionary Dr. Monique Rodgers. She is also the mother of Daniel Rodgers and Abigail Davidson. She is also a grandmother to seven beautiful grandchildren. She reared each of her children as a single parent and withstood the tests and trials as a mother. As the oldest daughter of four children, she learned the power of leadership at an early age. She is a licensed CNA and cosmetologist. She received an award from Wilford Academy for 1st place for the top hairstyle student in cosmetology. She also was a model for 10 years and created fashion clothing and designs while participating in numerous fashion shows. She spent 10 years working as a CNA from the age of 25. She is also a dynamic intercessor that has spent years birthing others in prayer and intercession. She lives a continuous lifestyle of prayer unto God. She accepted the Lord at the age of 20 and got saved. Amongst other notable ministry accolades she served as a Sunday school teacher and choir member. Apostle Rodgers endured many tests and trials but learned to withstand through prayer. She was a preschool teacher in 1992. She has survived numerous attacks from the enemy through the power of prayer and living a lifestyle for God. In 1997 she received the call to ministry. She has helped to groom several women and men in ministry and prepare them for the battle ahead. She has also taken several people into her home and helped them to get on their feet. As a survivor of domestic violence and homelessness her heart of service to God first and then to others is most notable. She also served as a pastor for Empowerment Word in 2009. In 2019 she also served as a Pastor for a local church in Marion South Carolina. She received an Associate's degree from the School of The Prophets in 2010. Apostle Rodgers was ordained as a Prophet in 2010 and in 2021 she was ordained as an Apostle. She is honored to participate with other notable intercessors in both her first book and collaboration as a best-selling author in Called to Intercede Volume One.

CHAPTER 17

Prayer Works

Most people would equate prayer as being a notion of where we only extend requests to God and wait for years to receive answers, however prayer is more than this in that it is the communication point of access that we have to our Father in Heaven Jesus Christ. It is the power source to our lives. I am a living witness that prayer works, in this chapter I will discuss how prayer has indeed worked for and has changed the trajectory of history for my children, grandchildren, family, siblings, friends, and for myself. Prayer has truly been one of my lifelines as it has helped me through some of the most difficult and pressing times in my life as a single parent. In 1 Thessalonians 5:16-18 it says, "Rejoice always, pray without ceasing, give thanks in all circumstances; for this is the will of God in Christ Jesus for you." Another is confession to God helps to give us a continual heart of forgiveness to God and to others daily. One of the most enduring times in my life was losing one of my daughters at the age of three months old to SIDS (sudden infant death syndrome). I thought that God had failed me the moment I lost my daughter and had to bury her. It felt like life was being ripped from the inside of me. I immediately began to pray after that day that God would give me a daughter that would bring joy to life.

During my next pregnancy with my daughter Dr. Monique Rodgers my little "Mo-Mo" there was something unique about this pregnancy in that I cried the whole time and was so depressed. My prayer became one like Hannah's in the Bible to which I asked God to give me a daughter that would be joy not only for my life but to the world. On August 2nd one of the greatest gifts that God could ever give to me was finally born and she did just that, bringing joy to my life and protection to my family and myself in ways most astounding. I am so grateful that God heard my prayer and that my daughter is now helping so many people. As a parent, I have spent my life in prayer for all my children. I was able to recognize all their callings and their gifts early in life and I understood that as the firstborn that God had chosen me to really birth out some things for my family. My prayer has always been that my children would go farther than I could ever go in life and that they would indeed make a difference to the world while serving God. Another time that I could remember God answering my prayer was when I encountered domestic abuse in my life from past boyfriends and even from my ex-husband who is now deceased. Prayer helped me to cover my family and to not give up before my breakthrough. There have been countless moments that I can recall when one of my children would call me and ask, "Mom, will you please pray for me?" My immediate response has always been yes for me as an intercessor. I look forward to every opportune moment that I can spend praying for someone else. Prayer is the communication point that we need to daily connect with and spend time with God lifting other individuals that need help.

There is a persistence in prayer that God wants us to be able to work to gravitate towards daily. We must first become consistent in our prayers and do not give up on God and understand that prayer really does work. There are three responses that God can give us which are: yes, maybe or no. In all three of the responses that may give to us it is according to his will that the decisions in prayer are being made. One of my favorite scripture passages that I can recall about God really answering someone in prayer was Daniel when he was in the lion's den. He could have been hopeless and afraid, but he was not because he has spent years with God giving him daily time in prayer three times a day. He was connected to God and therefore he had no fear. I also think about David and Goliath. David did not look like he could slay a giant with a sling shot and smooth stones, but he has been anointed and hand-picked by God and his lifestyle of trust and prayed to God showed up when he most needed it to. I would like to encourage every intercessor that has lost hope about prayer that prayer works and to never give up on prayer to God because he is a prayer answering God that will answer your prayers.

About the Intercessor

Yolanda Turner

Yolanda Turner has been called to be a teacher and an inspirational speaker. She is the Author of Morning Glory, a 52-week Devotional and Pocket Prayers, a collection of 100 Scriptures and Prayers.

In her continued service to God, she started a Women's Bible

Study Group called Ladies Adorned by Christ & Empowered

(L.A.C.E.). She is a certified Helpline Counselor Volunteer for the Crisis Services of North Alabama, and a member at the Fellowship of Faith Church, Huntsville, Alabama.

Yolanda is actively involved with the New Covenant Emmaus Community that serves the northern Alabama and southern Tennessee areas.

Minister Yolanda Turner attributes her success of being a wife, mother, grandmother and great-grandmother to her devotional time and Prayer-Life, which have kept her strong in faith and close to her Lord and Savior.

CHAPTER 18

Answering The Call:

Obedience Is Better Than Sacrifice

I was awakened from my sleep to the sounds of a woman's screaming voice. She was pleading for help. I perceived in my spirit that her life was slowly slipping away, brutally. The scream pierced through and shook me to my very core!

I continued to lie quietly in the darkness of my bedroom, waiting to hear any sounds the night might offer. But there was nothing, nothing, but silence. I drifted back to sleep, and soon after the horrifying sound of this deathly scream could be heard CLEARLY in my ears, again! My spirit was immediately sensitive to an overwhelming grief, as the screams continued. My initial thought was, "whose daughter am I hearing screaming for help?" It never crossed my mind that in all this, I was dreaming.

I reached over to shake my husband abruptly from his sleep. I needed him to confirm that the screams I was hearing were truly happening in real time. With a sense of urgency, I said, "Wake-up! Do you hear that?"

And of course, his response was, "Hear what?" My grief was intensifying. I replied, "A woman is screaming for help! Listen!"

In this darkness of the midnight hour or early morning, I wasn't sure, but this woman's cries were for certain. "I just heard her scream again! Did you hear it???"

How could he not? It was resounding in my ears.

"NO." But my question alarmed him. "Who is it?" He asked.

"I don't know but it's someone's daughter and her life is in peril." "Does her voice sound familiar to you?"

"No, I am not sure, but she's young and she is being attacked." How did I know this? Why were these words spilling off my tongue with such conviction? My husband's body slightly shifted, as to say, I'm right here. We listened, giving all our focus to the sounds of the night, straining to hear but nothing was heard.

"Sweetie, I believe you're just dreaming." I felt his body sink back into the comforts of our bed. "Why don't you go back to sleep." I agreed with him, so I attempted to refocus my mind, as my body lay rigid. I was sure this was different. Moments later I heard the command of the Holy Spirit, say, poignantly, "Get up and pray." It was assertive, strong, but resolved. Once again, the screams could be heard.

This time I understood that the plea for help was only heard in my spiritual ears! "Get up and pray!" The Holy Spirit had quickened my spirit to rise up and go into intercessory prayer. I wasted no time reporting to the battlefield. The grief I felt now transitioned to fight. This call to prayer was spiritual warfare, and the only way of breaking this conflict, this attack on this young woman's life, would come through my prayer. I leaned on the power given by Christ and the power of the Holy Spirit to stop this assignment ordered by Satan and to save her life through the authority of God's Word, being released in the Earth, and into her atmosphere!

I jumped out of my bed praying aloud in tongues, followed by, "No weapons formed shall prosper against her, no weapons formed shall prosper against her, and she will live and not die! Satan, you cannot have her life! She will complete all her Godly assignments here on Earth. Touch not God's anointed one. Satan, you cannot have her life!"

This fervent prayer was united with my husband's prayer as he quietly awoke and joined me. We prayed the prayer to bind up

Satan's evil attack meant to kill her. My husband followed my lead as I began to sing praises unto God!

Periodically, I would give an offbeat clap; this clapping was symbolic of every chain of destruction breaking. This fervent warfare of prayer and praise went on for about 40 minutes. Afterward, my husband gently touched my shoulder and asked me if I was good. I replied, yes, you can go back to bed. I remained up and continued to pray until I felt a release in my spirit to stop praying. When it happened, I received a word in my spirit - "It's Done." The peace in my spirit gave me "blessed assurance," as the writer states, "Perfect submission, all is at rest," and our prayers had been answered on her behalf. She will live!

I was able to go back into a peaceful sleep. Hours later, I was up and conducting my daily routine, not thinking about what had just transpired in the 3:00am O'clock hour. My day had come to closure without incident and off to bed, I went.

I was awakened to a ringing phone at 3:00am (precisely 24 hours later). My daughter struggled to talk after her voice had been severely injured; her abuser strangled her until she lost consciousness. She sustained broken nails, scratches, bloodshot eyes, and vocal cord bruising caused as she fought for her life, screaming for help! Physical scarring is still present. The emotional trauma had a long-term effect on her as well.

Praise Be To God, our daughter is delivered, healed, and actively serving and living for God's glory.

I know in my entire being that intercessory prayer that we prayed that night not only saved the life of our daughter but the lives of many daughters.' Please, understand the spiritual impact that intercessory prayer has on the body of Christ, family, and even strangers. I thank God for my obedience to answering the call of intercessory prayer! *"With all prayer and petition pray at all times in the Spirit, and with this in view, be on the alert with all perseverance and petition for all the saints." - Ephesians 6:18*

Even though I write this as my own testimony, my daughter shared something with me much later. She experienced a transition in her unconsciousness and when in "The Light" God lovingly and gently told her, "No, no my love, not yet." This was evidence that God used my prayers to distinguish between life and death!

About the Intercessor

Prophetess Ursula Lett Robinson

Ursula Lett Robinson is a gifted teacher and preacher who has a passion for the Word of God. She is a licensed and ordained elder and has a unique prophetic anointing that comes forth while teaching. She is a charter member of Priestly Praise Ministries where she serves Apostle Lee and Elder Priscilla Lyons. She is the founder of Reflective Word Ministries, a para-church ministry designed to equip believers to rightly divide the Bible. God has gifted her in several areas, and she uses those giftings whenever and however she is needed. She is a teacher, musician, singer, playwright, mentor, and author. Understanding that "to whom much is given, much is required," she is determined to fulfill everything that God has assigned for her to do. She loves to spend time with her husband, Maurice, and her family and friends. She enjoys cooking and whenever she has the opportunity, you will find her curled up with a good book.

CHAPTER 19

Ready, Aim, Pray

Now this is the confidence that we have in Him, that if we ask anything according to His will, He hears us. 1 John 5:14 NKJV

You have been asked to lead prayer for a women's conference, and there will be women from all walks of life there. Some attendees are on leave from the women's prison, and others are business owners or executives in their companies. Does it matter what you pray? What does it mean to be ready to pray? What would constitute readiness in this scenario? Maybe, the question should be, "have you given thought to what God desires"? God knew who would attend this conference, and He knew you would be asked to pray. He is entrusting you to pray according to His will. In other words, readiness requires thought and preparation. Readiness requires spending time in God's presence. Readiness requires studying God's Word. Readiness requires building your faith. You may ask, "what does readiness have to do with prayer, with intercession"? I'm glad you asked.

In general, prayer is a conversation with God. It is a means of sustained spiritual effectiveness. Prayer reveals purpose. Prayer opens the door to the supernatural and ushers in the presence of God. Prayer prepares, protects, and restores the "pray-er" and the "pray-ee." Prayer guarantees victory before the battle is even fought. Prayer produces a change in people and circumstances. Prayer is an essential part of the armor of God (see Ephesians 6:18). Intercession is a specific type of prayer. The Hebrew root word that is often translated as intercede is paga. Paga means to meet, attack, strike or cut down. When you intercede, you are an intermediary between God and man: a go-between, gap-filler, hedge builder, or stronghold destroyer. An intercessor is contracted by God to speak to Him on behalf of another. An intercessor is equipped to access Heaven's resources to meet, attack, strike or cut down to manifest the will of God in the earth realm, and this access occurs through prayer.

Let's look at Jesus. Jesus prayed so often that His disciples did not ask Him to teach them how to work miracles; they asked Jesus to teach them how to pray. Jesus modeled prayer and the sacrifice of praying. They saw Him pray before and after ministering. They realized that He rose early and would find a quiet place to pray (see Mark 1:35). They recognized the connection between His prayers and His power. Intercession requires sacrifice. God may wake an intercessor in the middle of the night to pray even though He knows that the intercessor must go to work the next day. You may have planned to go to the mall, but you cannot get out the door.

You feel a tugging in your spirit to pray for someone or for a situation. Intercession is target specific. In other words, when God calls you to intercede, there is a bullseye you must hit every time. So, how do you learn to hit the bullseye? You must first keep a pure heart through repentance. Secondly, you gain confidence by spending time in His presence, praying in faith, and expecting God to move on your prayers. You sit and listen to what He has to say, and then you pray what He said. Thirdly, hitting the bullseye requires faith! You must believe God. You must believe that God can do the impossible. Lastly, you must study the Word of God and declare His Word. God said in Isaiah 55:11, "So shall My word be that goes forth from My mouth; It shall not return to Me void, but it shall accomplish what I please. And it shall prosper in the thing for which I sent it." His Word always produces!

The Kingdom of God is voice-activated. He demonstrated voice activation when He spoke the worlds into existence. He made us in His image and likeness and equipped us with the same ability to activate life just as He did. That time spent with God enabled Jesus to always do His will. Likewise, when we spend time with God, He speaks His heart and mind to us, and we can then pray for His desire to be manifested. Now, you are prepared to stand before that audience at the women's conference. You are ready. You have already interceded, and He has given you the words to speak, so now take aim and pray!

About the Intercessor

Darlene Williams

Darlene Williams is a single mom of five who loves God. She was born and raised in Chicago. She is an Evangelist, Author, and Motivational Speaker.

She is very passionate about helping others, especially youths, because of the many things she dealt with as a youth growing up.

She has a passion to one day start a prison ministry working with adults and youths that are incarcerated.

She does also plan on having a podcast soon as well to have others who have been abused to be comfortable in telling their story and getting healed and set free from trauma and pain that is buried on the inside.

CHAPTER 20

The Eyes Of An Intercessor

Being an Intercessor is a very big responsibility, yet it has its fulfillments. Many don't really understand the role of an Intercessor. They are the ones God calls and uses to stand in the battlefield against the enemy for God's children. His children mean a lot to him, and it saddens him when they find themselves in battles they can't seem to win.

His children don't know that he loves them so much he even sent his own beloved son, someone He cared for so much to help them. Someone he allowed to be crucified to death, to become our redeemer. That's funny though because some of his children don't even seem to care about his great sacrifice. They tend to side with their enemy who wants to destroy them out of jealousy because of the love God has for us. Yes, Satan is our enemy.

Yet In spite of this, God still cares anyway for his children. Wow, that's a deep love, and who can beat the love of the Father? So now he has to raise up Intercessors who can help him tend to his children like a shepherd does their sheep. So, he begins to create them and raise them up before they are in their mom's womb. Now they won't remember the instructions given before birth. But they will have a certain desire on the inside for souls.

They won't be like others with just plain eyesight. Their sight will see what God can see about that person. An ordinary person will see that person as a hardheaded child who seems to keep acting out!

An eye of an Intercessor will see the hurt, broken child who is suffering trauma wounds that needs healing, but they don't know how to fill the void or fix it. It's like God gives Intercessors these special hero glasses that beep when they need to go fight the enemy for one of God's children.

While someone else may think they are crazy or may tend to get away from them. An Intercessor can see the spiritual chains wrapped around his body or mind and goes instantly into warfare prayer concerning that person's wellbeing. The Intercessor has eyes like an eagle that can see far into the enemy's camp!

They can tell when the devil is trying to bind someone's mind, heart, will, finances, children, family, business, etc. and they instantly go into the enemy camp in the spiritual realm in prayer, fasting, or praise for that person, nation, family, etc.

Now don't get me wrong, their job is not easy. And it comes with many fiery trials. They also don't just know how to use their spiritual eyes. They first have to go through combat training! They have to learn how to use their gifts and discernment to see the traps of the enemy for others. But first they have to learn how to discern the traps among themselves and their families, etc.

After their last test, which turns into testimony, they become equipped to go into battle in prayer and fasting for that lost soul or their person or child. The eye of Intercessor must stay sharpened to catch the devil's traps. Remember the Bible says he is like a lion walking back and forth trying to see who he can devour. Therefore, their eyes have to stay on point. So, if you ever run across an Intercessor, please don't take them lightly!

Know that those eyes they have on their faces can take them way beyond what we can see. It can help them see the traps of the enemy in his camp and you best believe they are getting ready to get in combat mode to fight for that soul or souls behalf for their Heavenly Father. Those are the eyes of an Intercessor.

About the Intercessor

Pastor Clara-Cohee Russell

Pastor Clara Cohee-Russell: Founder & CEO of REACH Women 4 God Ministries, which is now Women Walking In Wisdom. She is a woman after God's own heart, called and chosen by God to preach the word of God in the highways and byways; reaching out to a dying world sharing what thus says the Lord. She is a prayer warrior, an exhorter, mentor, certified transformational life coach, worshipper, Entrepreneur, and three-time published author.

Pastor Cohee-Russell worked as an Evangelist serving in ministry since she was a young child growing up in the C.O.G.I.C. background, singing in the choir, teaching Sunday School, and singing on the Praise Team. Pastor Russell was saved at the early age of 5 years old, she was saved and filled with the Holy Ghost with the evidence of speaking in tongues at the age of 13. Pastor Russell was totally sold out to Christ at the age of 28 years old and began working in full capacity.

Pastor Cohee started working as a servant in her church where she served for 19 years in different auxiliaries, a faithful choir member and praise team member and worked in clerical positions and she answered her call as an Evangelist and is now serving as Assistant Pastor in ministry with her husband who is the Pastor of Iron Sharpening Iron Ministries.

Co-Founder/Administrative Officer of Iron Sharpening Iron Ministries 501c(3)

Founder/CEO Butterfly Life Mentoring & MNM Coaching

Founder of The Praying Mothers of Inmates Prayer Ministry

Founder/CEO of Women Walking In Wisdom

President of Precious Sister Women's Ministry

President of WCC Women's Ministry

Volunteer Coordinator over Helps Ministry

Church web site coordinator

Praise Dancer & Drama Team

Praise Team Leader

Choir Member and Secretary

Intercessory Prayer Team

Sunday School Teacher

VBS Teacher

Hospitality & Usher Board

President of Sunshine Band

Chair Person of MLH Scholarship Committee

WCC

Pastor Russell later was married Oct. 16, 2010 upon which her and her husband Pastor Harold Russell began to operate in their callings from God together. Shortly after their marriage God birthed a Women's Ministry in Pastor Cohee-Russell which is still being molded into a final work for the Lord; Pastor Cohee-Russell has served as a Sunday School Teacher, she served as President of WCC- Women's Christian Council, where she hosted her first women's conference which was a great success in the Lord in 2012.

She has served on the Praise Team and as a Choir member and served on the Missionary Board.

Pastor Cohee- Russell was licensed as an Evangelist and worked as unto the Lord doing street ministry, feeding those who are less fortunate and the homeless, handing out personal hygiene bags and going into the prisons teaching and preaching the word of God.

God elevated Pastor Cohee-Russell and her husband Pastor Harold Russell to Pastors of ISIM (Iron Sharpening Iron Ministries) with boots on the ground. Carrying the word, giving clothing, hygiene bags and food to those on the street corners in the parking lots, sharing the word to those in the prisons, in the juvenile detention centers and wherever God leads, being true foot soldiers for Christ.

CHAPTER 21

When a Mother Prays

I grew up in a small town in Texas, where people actually sat out on the porch and waved at friends and neighbors as they passed by. Well, I have always been what people would call a church girl. My mother kept my siblings in Church most of the time. So, singing and giving God praise was a natural thing to me. However, prayer was only performed by the preacher, ministers, or missionaries. I served faithfully in Church as I got older. My responsibilities included:

- Being an usher.

- Sunday school teacher for the toddlers.

- Helping with the Sunshine Band for the more minor children.

- Cooking dinner for special church services.

But again, praying was not one of the things I actually did in the Church. I did, however, have a prayer life at home. It was short and sweet prayers; little did I know they would soon be more than that.

As I grew up into my young adult life, I encountered real-life problems and situations.

As I knew it as a young child, life was no more. My mother died when I was sixteen years old, and my siblings all were married and moved away. My Dad remarried and left me alone in the house I grew up in. He was still there in town; whenever I needed him, all I had to do was call him, but at the same time, I was alone. As I grew older and made grown-up decisions for myself. I decided to move to a larger city not too far from home but far enough that I would have to learn to navigate on my own in life.

Although I say on my own, God was always with me, I just didn't realize it yet. I found myself working, paying my own bills, and making my way. Still, I was in a relationship that really would never go anywhere, even though I thought he was going to be my husband. We would have children and live a wonderful life. Well, how many of you know that is not how things worked out?

About the Intercessor

Marian Murphy

Marian Murphy is the author of "T.E.A.R.S." and is the strategy God used to heal the grief of losing my only son through Trust, Endure, Adhere, Restore, and Stand. I am co-author of "Called to Intercede" collaboration. I am a mother of 3 children, 6 grandchildren, and 1 great-grandchild from North Carolina. I am a licensed Cosmologist, and owner/founder of a non- profit organization called "Compassionate Womb" to assist grieving parents while providing baskets with stress balls, bubbles, grief journals, comfortable socks, blankets, stress release candles, massage vouchers, manicure and pedicure vouchers, Bluetooth colors speakers, etc. to help them to release on a daily.

I provide grief presentations and services to educate churches about the grief stages and how to handle them with tender, love, and care.

I have an educational program on the health and wellness of grief. I graduated as Cum laude with a Master's Degree in Human Resources and Public Administration from Strayer University.

CHAPTER 22

Holy Spirit Unlock All of the Pain through Your Intercession for Me

Have you ever been extremely hurt by the people whom you never thought would inflict such deep pain on you? Many types of pain are sent from the enemy with the intent to kill you.

The first thing we must do daily is pray to our Father as He gives us His assignment from Him. Prayer is what draws us closer to our God. God desires to use us to intercede when He speaks to us. We must allow Him to pray through us as His vessels. There are many hurting people who has been wounded by betrayal, divorce, death of a loved one, car repossessions, loss of a job, relationships, home foreclosures, miscarriages, drug addicts, illnesses, stresses, homelessness, etc. Oftentimes, the load can be so heavy that it causes us to lose focus on casting our cares upon the master who can resolve our problems. The enemy can cause us to attempt to take matters into our hands without consulting God for our answers, healing, resolutions, strategies, and guidance and release of cares and heart to the Father. We should always consult God before making decisions that could affect our lives. God has commanded us to "TRUST NO MAN." (Psalm 118:8)

How do you know that you are an intercessor? When you place God first in your life, He desires purity and for you to be a glory carrier. As we spend time in the presence of God, we are able to feel how He feels, we are able to be one with Him spiritually. Obedience is the key to be sensitive to His unction to pray about what concerns Him. God has awakened me in the middle of the night, and I could feel the pain of individuals I didn't know, to intercede on behalf of their situation. I get up and intercede for their situation. Oftentimes, God allowed me to pray in different heavenly languages. There are times when God will allow us to know whom and what we are praying for. However, there are times He will not allow us to know. When we allow the Holy Spirit to pray in our heavenly language through us, then we are totally yielded to our Father. God loves us so much that when we are so weighted down and can't pray, God uses others to intercede on our behalf or He will intercede for us through us. The most powerful prayers we can pray are when we use our heavenly language, because the enemy cannot interpret what we are saying, and he has no idea how to come after us. The prayer of intercession is our secret weapon to win the victories in our lives. As we allow the Holy Spirit to intercede for us through heavenly languages, we are able to conquer many battles that are sent to destroy our lives.

Many of us are called to intercede on behalf of people from other countries, and their leaders. It is vital for us to be obedient and persistent when God urges us to pray in that moment—it could be a life-or-death situation. An intercessor is a special, serious calling which cannot be taken lightly because we are held accountable for the life God has called us to intercede and stand in proxy for. Intercession is allowing the Holy Spirit to pray through us for situations that we may not know are coming. God uses our intercession as His secret weapon against the plan of the enemy.

God desires for us to be pure vessels as we exemplify His love in our lives daily. We must surrender our wills to God, allowing Him to lead and guide us directly into our purpose. There are times when the pain is so deep that we can't pray. This is when we must invite the Holy Spirit into our hearts to intercede on our behalf as we trust Him to heal our wounds. Praying in our heavenly language is a gift, because even when we don't know what to pray, the Holy Spirit does, and He will intercede for us.

God even understands our tears as they are prayers as well. God collects our tears to water the seeds planted and to flourish through us. It is vital to spend time in God's presence as we allow Him to purge and cleanse our hearts for purity. Psalms 56 tells us that our tears travel to God as prayers when we can't pray. I am a living testimony that there were many days when I could not pray, and I had to trust that God understood the pain and prayers in my tears. He wiped them from my face as He made intercession on my behalf. There were times that I didn't know what to say, but called on the name of Jesus, praying in my heavenly language. During the most difficult time of my life, I've learned that the best weapon and strategy that we can use against the enemy is our heavenly language or silent tears because only GOD can interpret these prayers. The enemy doesn't understand what we are praying for. Therefore, he doesn't know how to attack us to take us out. When we are in this posture and place with God, we become the conquerors and overcomers that God created us to be.

We are commanded by God, to pray without ceasing and called to worship Him in spirit and truth. As we worship, we are developing a personal relationship with our father which is most important. Worship is our place of protection from the fiery darts sent from hell against us. The enemy uses those who are closest to us to attack us but remember, victory is ours from this day forward if we adapt to the strategy of allowing God to use His secret intercession for us as we receive His love and healing power. Let us teach our children how to become overcomers and walk in complete victory.

About the Intercessor

Tyneise Seaborough

Tyneise Seaborough serves faithfully as a minister of Branded Hearts Church in Savannah, GA, where she is submitted, licensed and ordained under the leadership of Pastors Kenneth and Denise Rouche.' She has served as the youth pastor for the past eight years before transitioning into her current role as the leader of the intercessory prayer team.

Apostolic Reformer. Fire initiator. Prayer General. Tyneise comes in the power of Elijah and the spirit of Ezekiel and releases the glory of God wherever she shows up. Creative miracles, signs, and wonders follow her ministry.

Tyneise comes from a dynamic lineage of ministers and intercessors. She's a publisher, author of four books, and Amazon bestselling author of two books.

CHAPTER 23

The Burden Of An Intercessor

I have been on the road for nearly twelve hours, after taking way too many bathroom and eating breaks to count, enduring two screaming and hungry toddlers. Now, we had finally arrived in Norfolk, VA, for Thanksgiving, a trip I'll never forget. Before leaving GA, I fretted about traveling this long commute while toilet training my toddler. It was beyond exhausting, but we did it.

It brought great delight to finally see the reward of our labor, my brother. The following day, we had great conversations, reflecting on our childhood about devious things we did to drive my father crazy and laughed at my brother's corny jokes. And then it hit me, a burden for my pastor. I could feel the pain and weight he was carrying concerning the ministry. In addition, I could feel his fiery desire for the building that we believed God for.

I slipped away to a room upstairs to begin to intercede for my man of God. I remember crying and groaning in the spirit realm for an extended amount of time. Bloodshot eyes, hair all sweated out, body drenched in sweat, but the assignment was completed. Afterward, I went back downstairs to spend time with my family.

This reminds me of those precious moments that the bible records when Jesus would slip away quietly in the middle of the night to spend time in prayer with His Father. What an honor it is to partner with heaven to see Matthew 6:10 (KJV) come to pass, which reads, "Thy kingdom come. Thy will be done in earth, as *it is* in heaven."

For me, intercession starts with a burden. Take Nehemiah, for example. He was deeply burdened by the Jews who had survived captivity. He mourned, wept, fasted, and prayed for days about the state of Jerusalem. Their walls were broken down, and their gates were burned. The Lord granted him favor with the king. And every need was supplied, and the walls were rebuilt.

Apostle Bryan Meadows reveals in one of his teachings that all prayer begins with a burden and describes the process of prayer below:

Burden →Prayer →Expectation → Faith → Work → Collaboration → Miracles

I've never really given too much thought to the entire process of prayer, but I can definitely see how this transpires.

In these times, the Lord will allow us to feel others' burdens. He will then partner us with the Holy Spirit, our teacher, and aid. He will assist us with capturing the heart of the Father and pray regarding His perfect will concerning a situation. Personally, I call Him my best friend and a midwife. He helps me pull down promises, strategies, and solutions from glory into the earth realm.

Romans 8:26 (NLT) "And the Holy Spirit helps us in our weakness. For example, we don't know what God wants us to pray for. But the Holy Spirit prays for us with groanings that cannot be expressed in words."

Over two years ago, a previous coworker asked people on social media to pray for her son dealing with cancer. I graciously said yes to praying on his behalf. Within a short period, his vitals began to drop drastically, and the MD had only given him a few hours to live. I continued to pray for him, believing God for his miracle. When I woke up in the morning, he had already transitioned. I was devastated! This was the child that not too long ago we were celebrating his coming with a baby shower...and now he's gone.

I left the house and commuted to see my clients. But I couldn't stop crying. I pulled into a parking lot to have a talk with the Father. "God, I'm no good. I can't stop crying. I can't keep going into my client's homes with bloodshot eyes. You've got to help me."

I was in such a low place. And I was broken. Later the Lord spoke these words, "There is an angel that has a vial in its hand that has the cure to cancer. Pray for that angel to be released into the earth realm."

On another occasion, I had a vision of demons having a meet-up. The leader had what appeared to be a whiteboard, and I saw the word "cancer" on it. These little imps began celebrating their assignment to make the people sick. I became disgusted about what I saw and heard. I knew that I had been given the mandate to come against it. I asked the Lord, "is he a prince?" The Lord said, "no, he's a centurion.

Catch this revelation. First, we ask for angels to be released into the earth realm. Secondly, we pray for warring angels who will fight in the heavenly and open up the way for this angel to breakthrough. Thirdly, begin to decree and declare that the cure to cancer is on the earth now!

This is the power of intercession and partnering with the leading of the Holy Spirit! It yields results and produces miracles! Pray through those burdens, intercessors!

About the Intercessor

Prophetess Deborah Arnold

Prophetess Deborah Arnold is the CEO of Deborah Arnold Ministries, a global ministry, founded on the scripture, Ephesians 4:11-13. Under the banner of Deborah Arnold Ministries, she is the Founder, CEO of Women of Purpose, Inc. With life experiences of divorce, rejection, low self-esteem, abusive relationships, being mentally, emotionally, physically abused and being spiritually wounded, she sought the Lord with a desire to help build women. Women of Purpose, Inc. was founded, and it now equips, encourages, and empowers women physically, mentally, emotionally, spiritually, and financially to fulfill their God given purpose in life.

With over 30 years in Ministry, Prophetess Deborah purposes in praying, prophesying, preaching, teaching the word of God. She flows in several gifts of the spirit including laying on of hands, impartation for receiving the Holy Spirit, healing and deliverance and miracles. She hosts virtual and in person services and events, including prophetic prayer meetings, prophetic prayer breakfasts, ladies' retreats, healing and miracle conferences, revivals, workshops, and seminars.

Prophetess Deborah has served in various capacities in church and leadership positions, including Armorbearer, Director of Intercessory Prayer, Director of Altar Evangelism, Director of Recreation Ministry, Small Groups Leader, Sunday School Teacher, Preaching Sunday Morning Services and Mid-Week Services. She has been ordained and operates in several of the 5-fold ministry gifts including, Apostle, Prophet, Evangelist and Teacher. She attended Blissett Temple True Church of God, Believers Temple Word Fellowship, Kingdom International Institute School of the Prophets and currently attends Influence Church.

Prophetess Deborah graduated from Scott Central High School. She earned her Bachelor of Science in Recreation Therapy at Southeast Missouri State University. She is currently employed by SSM DePaul Hospital Behavioral Health as a Recreation Therapist. Prophetess Deborah is the Founder, CEO of PurposeBound4Life, a coaching, mentoring, and consulting organization. She is a Certified Life Coach, a Certified Mental Health Coach, a Licensed Real Estate Agent, and a Licensed Life Insurance Agent.

Prophetess Deborah was a preacher's kid (PK) born in rural Morley, Missouri. She has been married for (32) years to Leon Arnold. They have two adult children, one son, Leon III who is 29 and one daughter Bianca Nikole' who is 23 years old.

CHAPTER 24

Created with a Purpose to Intercede

Have you ever felt a burden or urge to pray for the lost, for someone experiencing pain or suffering, a loss, an illness, or a financial need? Have you ever felt in your heart that God has called you to pray for others?

If you answered yes to either of these two questions, God wants you to know that he created you with a purpose to intercede.

What is an Intercessor? An Intercessor is someone who intervenes on behalf of another, through prayer. This is called Intercession or Intercessory Prayer.

The Bible is filled with examples of intercession including Moses, Abraham, Daniel, and Elijah who were God's Intercessors. They interceded on behalf of the people and God responded, forgave their sin, and helped them.

The Ultimate Intercessor is Jesus Christ. Romans 8:34 *"who is he that condemneth? It is Christ that died, yea rather, that is risen again, who is even at the right hand of God, who also maketh intercession for us."*

As Intercessors, we must first draw near to God, through our relationship with him, with our prayers, our worship, and our communion with him.

Have you ever noticed that when you love someone, you desire to spend time with them all the time?

If we genuinely love God, our desire should be to spend quality time with him. God loves us and desires to commune with us. One of the most effective ways to commune with him is through our prayers.

In seeking him for our desires, His desires become our desires, and he leads us into a place of intercession.

As I reflect on becoming an intercessor, I am reminded of my childhood. My Father was my Pastor; therefore, we were required to attend all church services, including prayer.

I can vaguely remember these prayer times. Everyone, including children, got down on their knees to pray. While on my knees, I was not praying the whole time, because I really did not know how to pray. My prayers would be, "Lord, forgive me for my sins, and please don't let me go to hell." Then I would spend the remainder of the prayer time talking quietly to my sisters.

At the age of fourteen, my father passed away. Everything in my life came to a halt. The reality of death became real to me. I felt numb and alone. It was exceedingly difficult for me to accept that my father was gone. I lost a father, a Pastor, a protector, and a provider. It changed my life and left a void.

I continued to attend church with my mom, but without my father, life was not the same and neither was church.

When the time came for the word of God to be preached, my oldest brother, a Deacon, would stand before the congregation and minister a short, but anointed message from Revelation 21:8. He would say "If you don't get saved, you're going to burn in a lake of fire and brimstone, forever and ever." This message imparted into my heart, a lifelong desire for salvation, a reverential fear for God, and a prayer life.

As I recall my life as a teenager in high school, and as a young adult in college, I was not walking with the Lord. I always felt like there were limitations on the things I could do. I knew God was watching me, and I felt convicted. When I committed sins, I was quick to pray a prayer of repentance "Lord, forgive me." I knew God was not pleased with my life.

One day, while at home on a break from college, I was introduced to Intercessory prayer. I was awakened by my mom in the early hours of the morning. I heard her crying and interceding on behalf of her children and grandchildren. She was an Intercessor.

By the time I reached thirty, I was married with one child. God began drawing me toward him, so I rededicated my life back to the Lord. I started attending church and, within a year, accepted the call of God on my life to preach the gospel. Attending prayer meetings was One of the requirements for those called to preach.

I started attending prayer meetings, listened to others pray and prayed with them. I did not always know what to pray, but the Holy Spirit would pray through me.

Romans 8:26 *"Likewise the Spirit also helpeth our infirmities: for we know not what we should pray for as we ought: but the Spirit itself maketh intercession for us with groanings which cannot be uttered."*

As I continued in my prayer time, I noticed my prayers were being answered. My confidence to pray and ask God for anything increased, as did my passion for intercession.

I understood my prayers of intercession could go places I could not. My prayers of intercession could be offered as a gift, during times when I did not have anything to give. My prayers of intercession could serve others who had prayer needs. My prayers of intercession were an opportunity for me to stand in the gap.

Intercession is an assignment and our responsibility as a child of God.

1 Timothy 2:1 *"I exhort therefore, that, first of all, supplications, prayers, intercessions, and giving of thanks, be made for all men."*

In this hour, there is a clarion call! God is calling Intercessors, Prophetic Intercessors, Prayer Warriors, and Gap Standers. He is calling the young into position, and the old out of retirement! He is calling you to the forefront. He is calling you to stand in the gap, to make intercessions for your country, your nation, your government, your cities, your churches, your communities, and your families. He is calling you to wage war against the enemy through warfare prayers. He is calling you to prophetically decree and declare his promises in his word.

Intercessor, come forth! Your Purpose is calling you and your Destiny awaits you! You were created with a Purpose to Intercede.

About the Intercessor

Tracey L. Ricks

Speaker *Author* *Entrepreneur*

Tracey L. Ricks, better known as Lady T, was born in New York City and is the mother of three adult children and two grandchildren. She recently retired after 32 years of State Service and has now relocated to Houston, Texas. Tracey walks in her evangelistic calling, and her powerful testimony of deliverance from drug addiction, domestic violence, sexual perversion (lesbianism) in and out of the church, has encouraged many in their walk. Tracey is a published author of three books and has been blessed by the Lord to be gifted in writing poetry. *"If You Can't Say It – Let Me Create It"* is where Tracey creates original works of poetry for any occasion. Tracey loves to bake, and *Tracey's Tasty Treats* consists of various personal size cakes. Tracey loves encouraging souls and doing marketplace outreach evangelism. She relates well to young people and was previously the teen ministry coordinator for 11 years. Tracey desires most for her life to please the Lord Jesus Christ, and to be a blessing to His people. She is a member in good standing at Greater Grace Houston, under the awesome leadership of Bishop EL Usher and Co-Pastor Lady Tawanda L. Usher.

CHAPTER 25

What Do You Say, When You Cannot Pray?

When there is a calling on your life to travail and intercede for others, not only is it a calling, but did you know that it is also a mandate from God? At times it may not seem too difficult to go before the throne of God and intercede on behalf of your spouse, your children, your family members, your leaders, your church and even for those that you do not know in other states or countries. The word "pray" is listed in the Bible 121 times, "prayed" - 68 times, "prayer" - 106 times, "prayers" - 32 times, "praying" - 36 times and "prays" - 12 times, for a total of 375 times.

We know that it is absolutely imperative that we pray! In Matthew 26:40, we see where Jesus was going through and was looking for the disciples to be in prayer with Him and for Him, but what happened? Jesus found the disciples asleep. Jesus went and prayed, and came back again the second time, and when He came back, they were asleep again! After the third time Jesus told them to go on and take their rest. How many times have we purposed in our heart to pray, but wound up falling asleep? I know, this book is about being called to intercede, but what do you say when you cannot pray?

I've heard it said before that the very thing that we are called by God to do, is the exact area where the enemy is going to attack us the most. In times past, I was always told that I needed to pray, but was never really taught how to pray. "Praying is just talking to God" is what I was told, and although that is very true, we also must pray the Word of God so that our prayer will be effective. But what happens when life hits us, and we find it hard to pray? Or when we get complacent and instead of reaching out to talk to God when He first wakes us up, we reach for our phones instead?

Don't you know that 1 Peter 5:8 says, *"Be sober, be vigilant; because your adversary the devil, as a roaring lion, walketh about, seeking whom he may devour."* We must know that it is the plot, plan, and assignment of the enemy to have us lose focus; to cause us to not want to pray and go higher in our relationship with God! We cannot be ignorant to satans' devices, and we must push through in prayer! Have you ever heard the term, "PUSH – Pray Until Something Happens?" If you don't have words to say, shout unto God with a voice of triumph! Pray in your heavenly language, knowing that the Spirit of God is making intercession for you!

The reason I share this with you is because there was a time in my life when I was in this place. The enemy tried to keep me bound with a spirit of prayerlessness. I had to decree and declare that no weapon formed against me shall prosper, and let the devil know that the Lord gave me my mouth to praise and worship Him! I had to come to a place in my life where I knew without any doubt that I was going to be unmuzzled, pray and give God the glory!

One of the reasons why prayer is so important to me is not only the mere fact that God commands us to pray, but because prayer will definitely strengthen your relationship with the Father. When we are called as intercessors, it is because God has equipped us to go into realms and regions, and tear down demonic strongholds. *"For the weapons of our warfare are not carnal, but mighty through God to the pulling down of strongholds."* (2 Corinthians 10:4) There are strongholds, not only in our lives or in our families lives that need to come down, but all over this world. People are dealing with demonic principalities and powers that we, who are called to be intercessors, must contend with.

Is it going to be a fight? Yes! Is it going to be difficult at times? Yes! However, Galatians 6:9 says, *"be not weary in well doing for in due season we're going to reap if we faint not."* We are more than conquerors through Christ who loves us! So, what do we say when we cannot pray?

We shout unto God, we pray in our heavenly language and then, in an audible voice, we rebuke the devil and tell him to go to hell, because we will open our mouths and we will not be muzzled!

Ashlee Marie

Professional BIO:

Mother of 2 Beautiful Daughters

Military Advocate

Diversity, Equity, Inclusion Trainer

Public Speaking Certification

Certified Professional Christian Coach

Global International Speaker

UK + India + Canada

CEO of Naturally Purposed, LLC

Founder of A' Marie University

Built a Company with a baby on hip

Quit Full Time 9-5 Career

Coached 100+ Women Globally

EPIC 9-5 Exit Strategist

Podcast Host

Nominated Best Business Coach 2021

Best Selling #1 Amazon Author

Coach A' Marie focuses on clarity, career, and confidence! As an EPIC 9-5 Exit Strategist, she teaches women how to live life unapologetically and live life on their own terms. Many women desire to start a business and quite naturally fire their boss. As women we deserve to live life financially free and in control of our own time -- to spend with our families! Let's all be financially free.

CHAPTER 26

Rise Up & Boss Up

Greetings and blessings! I am Coach A' Marie! AKA Ashlee Marie, and I am a transformation coach who inspires women to challenge every area of their life that needs improvement! As an intercessor, it is essentially critical in this hour to hearken to the voice of God and obey his commandments. When I think back to being called to intercede, I often reflect on the days I spent in my birthplace, Houston, Texas! My amazing grandparents taught me how to pray and build a relationship with God. Our days were always filled with music, dancing, and laughter! My parents drove halfway across the country each summer to unload my two siblings and me into a city filled with bright lights and tons of love! As my parents unloaded the car with our luggage, I ran down the street and banged on my grandparent's door. They always opened the door with bags of coins and plenty of fresh vegetables that needed to be cut, cleaned, and cooked! In these moments, I listened to my grandmother share her thoughts about her God and the passion that she had in serving his people. I watched her bake cakes that ministered to the souls of so many and phone calls laced with prayers that moved mountains!

We prepared for Sunday dinner each Saturday night and most certainly laid out our Sunday Best outfits for an all-day church event. The services seemed to last for hours with what included never-ending altar calls and anointing oil! During the service, my grandmother worked graciously on the usher board along with the best aunt in the whole wide world to drape towels and sheets over those that sought deliverance and a personal touch from God! Before I wrap up this chapter, I wanted to share with you the stark difference between country living and city living related to life with prayer and life without prayer. Both are quite different, and with every moment spent with my amazing grandparents, I gained more knowledge about God's word and principles. My fondest memories of the city life in Houston, Texas, is that everything is fast paced, from the music to the fast talkers. We visited our other family members in the country. We enjoyed the freedom of silence and the ability to jot down thoughts of peace and journals filled with memories that would last a lifetime. A life filled with tons of prayer can yield a life of peace.

I learned a few lessons about intercession during this season in my life, and I pray that it encourages you to answer the call to intercede before this year closes! Covering another in prayer serves as a generational blessing in this season and in the seasons to come for that person's life. I've learned that the Holy Spirit drives you if you extend the invitation! There are times when I've arisen early in the morning and fervently prayed during the midnight hours. Next, I learned that prayer is powerful. Being intentional and consistent can fuel a flame even if it barely has a flicker. Finally, there have been different seasons in life whereby God speaks audibly. If we choose to listen, he guides and instructs us on just where he desires for us to go. This is so important to remember when he calls us the deep away from the safety of our familiar boat, family, and friends!

As I recall when God called me into the deep, I am reminded of my final days in corporate America working as a full–time employee. The days were laced with headaches, stress, and unfulfilling work. Yes, financially, I was well compensated, but inside I felt like I was called to do so much more! I challenged myself to devise a 12-18 month exit strategy to leave corporate and enter full-time entrepreneurship! Taking a leap of faith and walking away from a paycheck and solely depending on a faith check requires discipline, determination, and dedication. This inner work started years ago as a child and remains. Unknowing to me at the time, God was filling up the mental reservoirs that I would need one day to serve hundreds of women as they begin their journey to exit corporate America – transitioning from their paycheck palace to a faith check! The role of an intercessor is immaculate, awe-inspiring yet it is filled with a heightened sense of responsibility. Present-day, I feel called to intercede on behalf of faith-based women who seek freedom in all areas of their lives! Let's talk about the necessity for women to quickly understand their God-given purpose and the freedom to walk this out unapologetically!

This dedication and devotion have now given me the courage to lay prostrate before the Father and cry out as often as needed for my family and clients! As you flip through the pages, I want you to reflect on what inspires you to fight for those you love. Think about and all that is required to intercede on behalf of others. Who in your life needs a few moments of your prayer that will move a mountain? For me, it is those same grandparents that invested days and hours ensuring that I understood that God is a mighty God, and he still answers prayers. As I wrap up this chapter, I encourage you to concentrate on the areas of your life that need the most attention. Where in your life are you challenged or desperately needing to see God move? Even if life is hard, you can make it through to the end! Be mindful that God honors your yes.

About the Intercessor

Ashley Blanshaw

Singer, Songwriter, Music Producer, Solo Music Artist, Motivational Speaker, An Activist and Author

Facebook: Ashley Blanshaw

Facebook music artist page: Ashley Katisha Blanshaw

Instagram: @ashleylove509 and @iamashleyblanshaw

Twitter: @iamMsAshley

United Masters/YouTube: Ashley Blanshaw

SoundCloud: Ashley K. Blanshaw

Clubhouse: @ashleylove595

I am originally from Brooklyn, NY USA. I am a Singer, Songwriter, Music Producer, Solo Music Artist,

Motivational Speaker, An Activist and Author, Talk Show Radio Show Host. My singing and solo music career started at the age of 4 or 5 years old, Songwriting career started during my freshman year of high school and music career started during college years. I am author of 5 books: My Journey To Recovery and Inspirational with Ashley

Blanshaw and I am Determined, I am Determined Deluxe Edition and the HerStory Collaboration book. I have a talk show and radio show: Ashley's Inspirations and Inspirational Time with Ashley Blanshaw. I am an activist and advocate for mental health awareness. I am celebrating 21 years of being sober from mental health illness. I am in the process of becoming a mentor to people who struggled with mental health illness. I am the #LoveYourself Campaign for mental health illness. What gives me strength is my spiritual connection with God, my faith in God and my music connection.

Going through this mental illness battle for 21 years, I struggled with self-confidence, depression, and more negative things, but I realized that I have to encourage myself that I am beautiful, strong, empowered, more than a conqueror, a champion, a winner, overcomer, survivor!!!!! I am hosting my first national tour: The I am Determined Tour!!!!!!!

CHAPTER 27

The Anointing Of The Lord is Going to Break Every Chain

When we look at Isaiah 10:27, it says that the anointing of The Lord will destroy every yoke. It means that every evil plan that the devil has tried to put on you and try to put in your life will be destroyed. Also, every evil and negative curse shall be broken. It will be destroyed because it also says in Isaiah 54:17 that no weapon formed against you shall prosper. Point one: Always know that we serve a God that is a chain breaker. God is going to break and destroy every chain that has been holding you back, holding you captive and holding you in bondage. Every chain of depression, dark moments, loneliness, abandonment, rejection, obstacles, financial struggles, and bad relationships will be broken. You will break free from those chains that have been holding you back. Point two: Always know that the battle is not yours; it is The Lord's.

I know that there have been times when you have struggled to find a way out of your present situation. There were times when you started to wonder and keep asking yourself, why are you in this situation that you're in? I know there have been days when you were crying so much, you been worrying so much. There have been moments when you wanted to give up, you wanted to quit, and you wanted to throw in the towel. I'm here to let you know that God is going to make a way for you. He is going to fix the situation that you're in. God is fighting for you. God is working out that situation that you are going through. Just hold on and be strong, and don't give up. Get ready because the Anointing of The Lord is on the way. Point three: Get ready because your healing is on the way. God will heal you from every sickness and trauma that you have been experiencing. God will deliver you from all the negative things you are going through right now. God will restore you from all hurt and pain. Please know that God is your shelter in the time of the storm.

You might be going through heartbreak, depression, and dark moments right now, but we serve a God that will bring us out of them all. When we also look at Isaiah 54:17, it also says that "and every negative tongue, you will refute it." It means that every negative thing, every negative word that the devil has told you, is nothing but lies. Encourage yourself that you believe and receive everything that God says about you. Encourage yourself that you are who God says you are. Encourage yourself and tell yourself that you are not worrying about what the enemy told you. Encourage yourself that you are more than a conqueror, a champion, a winner, victorious, an overcomer, and a survivor. Remind yourself that you are healed, restored, and delivered. Keep on praying and having faith because the anointing is on the way.

Whenever you feel weak, the anointing will strengthen you. You will be able to overcome and make it through the battle of addiction that you are going through. You will make it through this. You are going to be healed from this. I know that there have been times when the obstacles and struggles made you question if God hears you. You've been overwhelmed because the devil has been messing with you, messing with you and everything connected to you. However, I want somebody to look the devil in his face right now, and I want you to tell the enemy that he has failed. I want to encourage you that God will never leave you or forsake you. God hears your prayers, and God is answering your prayers. I also want to encourage you that God will protect you from all danger and from all harm. God will make a way for you. The Anointing of The Lord is on the way. Your healing, deliverance, breakthrough, and victory is on the way. Get ready because your harvest is coming, and it will be greater than you can ever imagine.

About the Intercessor

Crystal J. Farmer

Crystal Farmer is from the south suburbs of Chicago and has always had a passion for creative writing. She is the author of the children's book "Tom McNulty and the Sugar Mutants" and self-help "How to Overcome Unhappy Hour in Your Marriage. She is married to her husband of 12 years and together they share 4 wonderful children with fun times and God as the foundation of their home. When not busy, she enjoys watching great movies, listening to music, and creating short films. Also, a graduate of the University of Phoenix Associate of Arts in Mass Communications. Altogether, her service to the world is to make an impact on the lives of the family through love, literacy, and creative arts while promoting Christ for many years to come.

CHAPTER 28

Intercession: A Navigation System

In the year, 2003 the hit movie Wrong Turn six people find themselves driving in the woods of West Virginia hunted down by a cannibalistic mountain man tormented and trapped all because they took the wrong turn. The Global Positioning System (GPS) tells you where you are on Earth but intercessory prayer positions and tells you where are in the Spirit. I'm sure those six hikers wish they had an active system working and as believers, it is time for us to navigate into the supernatural. Have you ever heard the phrase; 'he went left'? Or how about, 'he's just going backward' as to say someone had worsened. Guess what? Today is a new day for you, no longer will you feel like you are on the wrong side road lost or stranded. Somewhere down the road, if you went left or backward here are some scriptures and encouragement to drive you back into the heart of God. Now shout this into your atmosphere "I am on the right track!"

While operating a vehicle it is the law that our seat belts are fastened to avoid injury to the body. Intercessory prayer allows us to travel into different dimensions in the realm of the Spirit and you are going to need protection. While you are on this road trip into intercession the enemy may set before you a mirage or roadblock, warning sees a red "DO NOT ENTER" sign in the realm of the spirit. And let's park on highway Ephesians 6:11-17 *"Put on the full armor of God so that you can take your stand against the devil's schemes. For our struggle is not against flesh and blood, but against the rulers, against the authorities, against the powers of this dark world and against the spiritual forces of evil in the heavenly realms. Therefore put on the full armor of God, so that when the day of evil comes, you may be able to stand your ground, and after you have done everything, to stand. Stand firm then, with the belt of truth buckled around your waist, with the breastplate of righteousness in place, and with your feet fitted with the readiness that comes from the gospel of peace. In addition to all this, take up the shield of faith, with which you can extinguish all the flaming arrows of the evil one. Take the helmet of salvation and the sword of the Spirit, which is the word of God."* My God, we have more protection in the supernatural than in nature. Now say this with me "God, I thank you that I am fully equipped to carry out my kingdom assignment as an intercessor."

Where are you located in the realm of the spirit? Do you feel like you are on the right path of intercession? We must stay in the spirit for our prayer life to be effective. Ephesians 6:18 *"And pray in the Spirit on all occasions with all kinds of prayers and requests. With this in mind, be alert and always keep on praying for all the Lord's people."* Many times, the Lord has allowed me to see into the Spirit. I can remember sitting at a local coffee shop and into a trance, I saw a freckled heavy-set woman with grandchildren. The Holy Spirit revealed that she was a struggling single grandmother and needed relief financially and from the stress of raising her grandchildren. Or the time God showed me two cars plus a semi-truck about to collide. As a result, immediate intercession went forth making my petition unto the Lord that those vehicles did not touch. Believe right now that you know your authority and location in the Spirit for you are going to experience the supernatural like you never have before because you are seated in heavenly places with Christ. (Ephesians 2:6). This is for the intercessors that need to get back on track because you are called to the mysteries of God. I decree and declare that you are aware of the red "DO NOT ENTER" signs, and you will break the covenant with every unclean spirit and tormenting thought bringing it into captivity. Intercessor, you are called to stand in the gap for your bloodline and dig others out of those graves where you once lived. Your new day is now, and you are now fueled in the right direction, and you literally have your drive back right into the heart of God.

About the Intercessor

Apostle Darcy Burgess

Apostle Darcy Burgess was born in Brooklyn, NY to Elder Gordon Burgess and Evangelist Shirley Burgess.

Darcy's anointing to preach was first evident at a very early age. Her walk with the Lord began in the Church Of God In Christ where she was active in church leadership.

One of the leadership positions that she held was at Kings Memorial Temple Church of God In Christ.

The Prophetic Call!

As time progressed the Lord came to Darcy and said "I have called you to the Prophetic!" Darcy gave many excuses but the Lord began to use her undeniably in the Prophetic Ministry.

Darcy has always been a person of prayer. She currently Host A Weekend of Intercession, and has started Raising Up Spiritual Anna's School of Intercession and Mentorship classes. God is using Darcy to Equip, Build and Release Intercessors to become an Army of Intercessors and Glory carriers. Darcy released her first book in April of 2021, called So Ordered! Issuing Restraining Orders through Intercession. I'm thoroughly excited that God has allowed me to be a part of this Collaboration!

CHAPTER 29

"Use Your Words"

Parents or teachers, how many times have you told your children to "use your words?" I worked at a preschool, and we were taught to tell our preschoolers to *"use your words."* When a child wanted or needed something from us, most times they would cry, scream, hit, bite, or kick. We explained to them, if you "use your words," we can understand what you want, and you will likely get what you asked for. We redirected their negative behavior and developed their communication skills. What parent or teacher wants to hear someone whining to them when they could simply ask and receive? How different is your Heavenly Father?

Matthew 7:7-11 "Ask and it shall be given unto you; seek, and ye shall find, knock, and it shall be open unto you: For everyone that ASKETH receiveth; and he that seeketh findeth; and to him that knocketh it shall be opened. Or what man is there of you, whom if his son ask bread, will he give him a stone? Or if he ask a fish, will he give him a serpent? If ye then, being evil, know how to give good gifts unto your children, how much more shall your Father which is in heaven give good things to them that ask him?"

The Father wants us to learn how to use our words so he can give us what we are asking for. We often limit God when we pray, because we're not properly articulating what we want to say. Thinking about it like this, instead of asking we are begging, kicking, screaming, and having a temper tantrum. We feel as though God is not answering or even hearing us as we pray. The Bible promises God hears us and will answer us; but we must use our words and… ask!

"I will answer them before they even call me. While they are still talking about their needs, I will go ahead and answer their prayers!" Isa 65:24.

When we learn how to effectively use our words, there will be results! What if we could learn how to put words together that could precisely target what we need God to do? What if I did not pray abstract, religious prayers but prayers that had a mission? I believe this is possible. It's time to stop praying prayers aimlessly.

Philippians 4:6 KJV *"Be careful for nothing; but in everything by prayer and supplication, with thanksgiving, let your requests be made known unto God."*

Our prayer language has the power and ability to create a world that we can form when we pray and ultimately frame the course of our lives as well as others! See your words when spoken the right way. Tone is so important that people have given study to this. They are called Linguists. According to the University of Arizona, in their college of Social and Behavioral Sciences linguists are people who study language.

Do you ever wonder why we say "feet" rather than "foots"? Or what we do with our mouths to make a b sound different from a p? Or why do we rarely say what we mean? It is questions like these that intrigue the linguist!

Many people think that a linguist is someone who speaks many languages and works as a language teacher or as an interpreter at the United Nations. In fact, these people are more accurately called "Polyglots". While many linguists are polyglots, the focus of linguistics is about the structure, use and psychology of language in general.

Linguistics are concerned with the nature of language and communication. It includes the following sub-areas:

- phonetics (the study of the production, acoustics, and hearing of speech sounds)

- phonology (the patterning of sounds)

- morphology (the structure of words)

- syntax (the structure of sentences)

- semantics (meaning)

- pragmatics (language in context)

It includes exploring the nature of language variations, changes over time, how it is processed and stored in the brain, and how it is acquired by young children.

Understanding is the key to perfecting our language in relation to our intercession. Words are important! When we are interceding for someone, the intensity or silence of a word will help us break through and navigate in the spirit realm. The way you say some things will help you get the point across and the right results. Let's look at a few definitions as it relates to intercession.

Articulatory phonetics are used to initiate a change in the volume: loud, soft, bellowing, screeching, etc. We can learn when and if it's necessary to articulate when engaging in intercession. John 11:43 says: *"and when he thus had spoken, he cried out in a loud voice, Lazarus, come forth."* If it's not necessary to use forceable, loud language at times, why did Jesus do it when calling Lazarus forth? I believe Jesus was calling Lazarus from a far place! Lazarus was dead for 4 days; he was not in his body. He was in a dead place and Jesus let death know that He had the authority and power to do so! Jesus called loudly to Lazarus, and he heard Jesus and obeyed!!! Hallelujah! There is power in our articulation.

Semantics is the meaning and interpretation of words, signs, and sentence structure. It largely determines our reading comprehension, how we understand others, and even what decisions we make as a result of our interpretations. Simply put, it is the study of meaning as communicated through language. Semantics is important in Intercession— how we understand the words we use in intercessory prayer makes our prayers more effective: we ask specifically as we pray for an individual, nation etc. When we enter into spiritual warfare, the words we use are wielded with authority and passion, led by the Holy Spirit. We use the words He gives us, incorporating tones as our words flow thus, we witness the precise results the Holy Spirit wants to accomplish through us!

About the Intercessor

Prophetess Jameela White

Jameela White is a born-again Christian believer, servant, and follower of Jesus Christ. She has many years of experience serving and leading in various ministerial auxiliaries, ministries, and functions. Jameela has a calling by God and is licensed, ordained, and affirmed to function in the office of a Prophet. She has a burden to compel believers of God to mature into a deeper relationship with God through Christ Jesus. After serving in ministry for many years and seeing the dysfunction in the structural church, and watching many turn away from the faith, Jameela has a passion to encourage the people of God to establish and maintain a committed relationship with God regardless of what is going on in the world around us. Outside of ministry, Jameela is a mother of three children (young adults) whom she loves dearly.

Jameela is also a Nurse, Travel Nurse, International Bestselling Author, CEO, Entrepreneur and has a tax-exempt ministry where she has provided ministry and services to the local shelters, and the communities in need throughout the United States. Jameela is an advocate for prayer and has a motto she stands by "Prayer is not a mere convenience rather it is an essential element to every Christian believer's life." Jameela has endured many trials in this life and has perseverance and a determination that she will succeed at all that God has purposed for her to do in this lifetime and live a lifestyle of exemplified faith standing firmly on the Word of God with the understanding that nothing is too hard for God, with God there are endless possibilities. Matthew 19:26 But Jesus beheld them, and said unto them, "With men this is impossible; but with God all things are possible."

CHAPTER 30

Pray to Intercede

When the topic of intercession comes to mind, I cannot easily address it without first covering the topic of prayer. My personal experience with God was that my prayer life birthed intercessory prayer and the prophetic nature and calling within me among other spiritual gifts, calling and God given purposes. In short prayer is my communication with God. Prayer is also a time for me to worship and praise God. When I pray, I am fully submitted to God and completely transparent repenting for my sins and acknowledging my shortcomings and sinful nature in my flesh and asking for the will of God for my life be revealed, so that I in return will submit to my heavenly Father's will, purposes, and plans for my life. By praying in this manner, I am following the revelation in the Holy Scriptures of the Bible when the disciples asked Jesus in Luke 11:1 "Lord, teach us to pray, as John also taught his disciples."

My prayer time also consists of being still and quiet to hear the response of Holy Spirit. This way of prayer has drawn me closer and deeper in my personal relationship with God and allowed me to experience the various attributes of God firsthand and develop, a true authentic relationship with my Heavenly Father, which is growing, evolving, and maturing on a continual daily basis. I have also learned more about myself, the closer I draw to the maker and Creator of all things including me. During the lowest points in my life, I have experienced a great depth of fervency in prayer which allows me to experience a greater depth of the presence of God. This encouraged me to go even further and deeper into my personal time of prayer. Understanding from the above scriptures quoted that I must know the will of God which is in encapsulated in the Word of God to have an effective prayer life. Along with the other supernatural and spiritual benefits I experienced from enduring in my personal prayer life I also received a greater depth of what I refer to as the three components of prayer, which are:

Obedience

Discipline

Knowledge and Wisdom

Obedience is what fuels submission to God. Let us be honest if you are not going to obey the ways, statues, and plans of God then you are not going to yield yourself to Him. In my personal prayer time, there is an exchange from my will to God's will as a result a greater level of obedience is, obtained. It takes discipline to stay diligent in prayer, and to adhere to prayer on a consistent basis. Effective prayer also requires you to be a disciple, to be studious of the Word of God. Knowledge and Wisdom partner together because having knowledge of God's will, purposes, and plans is vital, however wisdom is as vitally important for correct application and implementation of knowledge obtained. Knowledge and Wisdom are also revelatory gifts that are most effective in prayer. For me, the revelatory gifts of Word of Wisdom and Word of Knowledge were birthed in my personal prayer life. While everyone does not have a calling to the office of a Prophet every Holy Ghost filled believer of Christ has a prophetic nature. Mastery of these components of prayer is what opens the door to intercessory prayer. The more submitted I became to Holy Spirit in prayer it allowed Him to lead and guide me to pray for others. The more obedient I became in my personal prayer life the more of a disciple I became which displayed through discipline and submission to God, making knowledge and wisdom readily available both at a surface level and through the supernatural revelatory gifts. Obedience and discipline are needed to beckon to the call of prayer and intercession when Holy Spirit gently nudges you in the middle of the night or the wee hours of the morning. Or when God calls you to fast and pray. Knowledge and Wisdom must be implemented when we engage into prayer and intercessory prayer, both in the physical realm and if you have the revelatory gifts of Word of Knowledge or Word of Wisdom. The concepts of prayer grow in a greater depth the more we implement prayer in our personal lives as a lifestyle. These concepts to prayer also keep us from mismanaging faith, and praying a miss, there are times when the sovereignty of God will be supreme in a circumstance or situation, and we must agree with that in order to keep us from being discouraged in prayer and intercession.

So, in closing I say unto anyone who has a calling to intercessory prayer, be diligent in your personal time in prayer, allowing for the concepts of prayer to grow in deeper depths within you, and for them to take you higher heights in your personal time of prayer. Become intertwined with God where you are not living life separated from Him. Learn through implementation of prayer how to dwell and remain in the secret place of God according to Psalm 91:1 He that dwelleth in the secret place of the most High **shall abide under the shadow of the Almighty**. Learning to dwell in the secret place of God will eliminate the need for recognition, accolades, and excessive affirmation which can paralyze or destroy the life of prayer and intercessory prayer. Finally, be encouraged to never cease in prayer, knowing your labor is not in vain. Our Heavenly Father is attentive to the voice of His children, and He desires for us to commune with Him. Your fellow brothers and sisters need your prayers, the Earth itself is moaning and groaning in travail for the sons of God to manifest. Always be diligent in your prayer and intercessory life. Follow the example and leading of Christ. Never stop praying, never give up on praying, never get lackadaisical in prayer. Luke 18:1 And he spake a parable unto them *to this end*, that men ought always to pray, and not to faint.

God Bless You Always

About the Intercessor

Leading Lady Krystal Henry

Krystal Henry is an author, motivational speaker, and success coach, who created "Campaign Comeback," a multi-dimensional coaching hub, offering solutions, strategies, and inspiration to a diverse clientele. She is often known for her innate ability to lead others "from what if," to "what is." Having overcome life-changing battles with covid, cancer, infertility, and much more. Krystal proves herself an unfeigned survivor, equipped to change lives, bringing about a "Believe Better" mindset. Krystal is the Leading Lady of Power of the Gospel Ministries, alongside her husband Rev. Redd.

Together they inspire the masses, on the trailblazing "Power Lift Podcast" a part of the Positive Power XXI Media family.

Krystal is the author of inspirational manuscripts: "The Elements of You" and the amazon best seller "Made to Lead Millions." She has also co-authored in the following

Amazon best sellers "Jumpstart Your Mind," "Success Chronicles, Volume One." "You Define Your Own Success" and "Let the Kingdomprenuer Speak!" all organic expositions of an authentic passion, for people.

Krystal has appeared on Late Night with Sherida Lovelace, the Red Room with Shay Samuels and The LeKeisha Mosley shows. She has been featured in ShoutOut Atlanta, The Wealthy Coach, Businesstry, and Head &; Soul Magazines. She has also appeared on the covers of Bookprenuer and Author Push Magazines. Her effervescent voiceframes her success as one of the Co-Founders of "The Success Tank" and founder of "Campaign Comeback" and "Made to Lead Millions" Clubs on Clubhouse.

Krystal Henry. Leader. Speaker. Philanthropist.

CHAPTER 31

Intercessors Arise

"But the end of all things is at hand; therefore, be serious and watchful in our prayers." 1 Peter 4: 7 (NKJV)

We do not know the time or hour of our departure on the Earth; therefore, work, pray, and do not delay what God has called you to! This chapter is a prophetic assignment to evoke the called and elected Intercessors to Arise! This section will bring you clarity, motivation out of stagnation, and the willpower to arise and take your place of your call and election. The chapter basis comes from II Peter 1 :10 (NKJV), which states,

"Therefore, brethren, be even more diligent to make your call and election sure, for if you do these things, you will never stumble;"

A call is a heavenly summons that requires your verbal response in agreement. An election is a divine appointment that requires your acceptance by operating and functioning in the authority released by Heaven. Get ready to respond and positively act towards the challenges presented in this segment.

An intercessor is a person elected by God to intervene on behalf of another through prayer. Their prayer alters the results of that person's actions and/or the assignment of their adversaries. When choosing to accept such a powerful call as this, you must understand that your assignments include interventions through the Holy Ghost! The position of an intercessor is profoundly severe, long-suffering, and being in a perpetual state of watchfulness is standard. Intercessors are not usually ordinated or considered a frontline position in the church. However, they are vital to the success and expansion of God's Kingdom.

Here are a few examples that will help you recognize your call to Arise as an Intercessor! These intercessor assignments can stop you in your tracks, disturb your sleep, cause spontaneous fasting, prophetic visions, interruptions by means of sounds, languages, smells, colors, symbols, numbers, and biblical revelations. Intercessors are taught by the Holy Ghost to accept these types of interruptions, intrusions, and pauses to bring forth breakthrough, victory, restoration, and redirection.

Your awakening, acknowledgment, or divulgence to your call and election can happen at any point of your relationship with God. God will also give you a weight, heaviness, and burden for prayer. When I have sensed a thought, vision, or strong impression to pray for a certain person, group of people, circumstances, or situations, then I know that Heaven has released my assignment. While in prayer God can remain silent or reveal more details for intercession and declaration. When we do not know exactly what to say we can reference Romans 8:26 (NKJV) which states, *"Likewise the Spirit also helps in our weaknesses. For we do not know what we should pray for as we ought, but the Spirit Himself makes intercession for us with groanings which cannot be uttered."*

This can indicate to the intercessor that their voice is a beacon of fervent prayer on demand by the Holy Spirit! The voice of the intercessor's supplications heard in the heavenly realms according to Psalms 130:2. Ask God to reveal and give you clarity of any experiences that you may have dismissed and ignored during His process of calling you to intercede. Once you have received assurance and the infallible response from Heaven then you can without a doubt give your verbal agreement to Almighty Father God! Once you have verbally accepted your call then you can apply your obedience which is better than sacrifice according to I Samuel 15:22. The action of actually praying when God releases the burden and weight of each assignment is the evidence revealed in the lives of those for whom you are interceding. Now that your contemplation is over, confusion has cleared, and your decision is evident. Get into your established position and arise as an Intercessor! Arise means to begin to become apparent, surface, occur, proceed, and emerge into your place of relevance. Let the list of Six strategies below help you gain strength, get into position and disciple others along your journey.

Inform your pastor or ministry leader of your call and election.

Study some of these biblical intercessors such as Jesus, Holy Spirit, Abraham,

Moses, Samuel, Elijah, Jeremiah, and Daniel.

Set up a set time and meeting space with the Lord.

Get a prayer journal near your bed, in your car, or something you can carry in a purse or bag at all times.

Ask God to reveal to you whether you are to join a company of intercessors or lead a company of intercessors.

Stay focused, diligent and pray without ceasing according to I Thessalonians 5:17.

Imagine a league of intercessors completing assignments worldwide occurring daily, weekly, and monthly because of their obedience. Now Arise and take your place of purpose!

About the Intercessor

Heather Hancock

Heather Hancock has been writing her entire life. Called as an intercessor at the age of 18, she's a seasoned warrior and thrilled to be one of the authors in this *Called to Intercede* collaboration by Dr. Monique Rodgers. She's currently an Editor & a Writer for Coffee House Writers. Heather's also a contributing author in a devotional series published on Restored By Love's online site - *Bathsheba* was released in December 2021. Other publications include being a contributing author in *The Survivor Memoirs: Childhood Sexual Abuse by Joanne Kimberly* (February 2021). Heather had three poems and two short stories published in *The Coffee House Writer's Anthology Book 1: Nonfiction & Poetry and Book 2: Fiction*, (December 2020). She is currently editing her Christian Contemporary novel with the goal of publishing it in 2022.

Heather lives with her husband and cat, Willow, in a small town in southwestern Saskatchewan, Canada.

Website:

https://heather-hancock.com/

CHAPTER 32

Hidden No Longer

"He has made My mouth like a sharp sword,

In the shadow of His hand He has kept Me hidden;

And He has made Me a sharpened arrow,

In His quiver He has hidden Me."

(Isaiah 49:2)

Intercession is a complex gift, and no two intercessors have the same gift mix.

Assignments come directly from the Holy Spirit, along with the discernment, weapons, and strategies necessary for victory.

As with any gift there are different types of intercessors, and the names and lists vary amongst believers. Every intercessor can hear the Holy Spirit's voice. For those that are prophetic, some are night dreamers and receive revelation that way, while others receive their revelation through waking visions.

Some prophetic intercessors are seers, meaning they can see into and interact in the spirit realm (but only with the leading, and guidance of the Holy Spirit). I am one of those intercessors but reaching this level has taken 35 years and counting. I started out standing in the gap for others in prayer. Then burden-bearing taught me how to discern on multiple levels, and I learned how to persevere in prayer until God said it was done.

There were promotions: I was a personal intercessor, then a national intercessor, a watchman, a gatekeeper, and a seer. That journey has taken 35 years and is still in process. There is a cost, but Jesus died on the cross for my sins. Whatever He asks of me, I will obey. He knows He can trust me. I have proven it on the battlefield countless times.

The enemy has been trying to kill me since birth. I came into this world at 25 weeks gestation, weighing 1 lb. 6 oz. There were no NICUs when I was born. I breathed from moment one - my premature lungs were inflating by a miracle of God. I lived when doctors told my parents I would not. I thrived when doctors wanted to put me in an institution. I have overcome every obstacle set against me as a woman with Cerebral Palsy. The cross that I carry is one of suffering. I live my life inside the Refiner's fire.

Now, let me be clear - Jesus IS my healer. The timing of that healing is His alone. I have been prayed for thousands of times and will be prayed for again. I have faith and I do not have any hidden sin. The fact that I am not healed is because He is glorified through my suffering and the fruits of perseverance, tenacity, and dependency on Him. I am weak in the physical, but in the spirit, I am a seasoned, lethal warrior. Nothing restricts me in that realm. My spiritual form is free to do His bidding.

The house I lived in from the time I was born until age eleven was "haunted." Of course, I know now that it was demonized. I was battling with the spirits in that place at a young age. Traumas, abuses, and intense bullying led to me planning my suicide by the age of fourteen. Jesus ran to me and saved me literally and spiritually before I could carry those plans out.

He called me as an intercessor at the age of eighteen. I knew I prayed differently than others, but it all came to a head at a church camp during a senior co-ed week where all hell literally broke loose. The summer of 1986 was a spiritual warfare 101 course by fire. Not literal fire, spiritual fire. Something rose up in my spirit and came pouring forth with power. There was no way any demon was getting near the teenagers in my cabin. I was the warrior at the door, with sword in hand and armor in place. The voice of the Holy Spirit became crystal clear as He gave me the strategies that prevailed. One intense night of darkness resulted in half of the teens at that camp giving their hearts to Jesus. To God be the glory.

Since then, I have prayed with other intercessors to hold ground won for the Lord. I have taken ground back in the spirit realm as a gatekeeper over a geographic area, and now I am His seer. I see clearly in the spirit realm and petition the courts of heaven when directed to do so by the Father. Every promotion has begun with Jesus upgrading my armor, including the swords that I carry.

Let me share one part of one of my waking visions with you. I always enter intercession through praise and worship. One day, something new happened... my body stayed in the den where I was praying, but my spirit entered the realm for the first time as a seer.

"I found myself in the midst of a glade in a forest. My blue and silver sword was in my hands and I was in a defensive stance, aware of the wolf pack circling me. A lone silver wolf, with ice-blue eyes, approached me. Instantly I knew what to do! I raised my sword over my head with both hands around the handle and the blade pointing down. In one swift movement, I drove the blade of the sword into the ground. A wave of silver light rolled outward in all directions from where I stood. I looked up and watched as every single wolf dropped to the ground, and rolled belly up in submission. Jesus was standing behind my right shoulder and moved to stand in front of me. I knelt before Him and He removed my armor piece by piece, replacing each one with a new one. "Receive this upgrade, my daughter." He said, as he put a new sword in my hand. The vision ended and I was back in my den."

I knew I was no longer hidden. A huge adjustment with lots of resistance because I have been called out for this season. Our Lord Jesus is returning and there is work to be done!

About the Intercessor

Minister Andrea E. Monroe

Andrea E. Monroe is first and foremost a child of God. She is a minister of the Gospel of Jesus Christ. She is a Kingdom entrepreneur. One of her gifts is making the Word of God applicable and personal to you. She is a healing intercessor and international speaker.

Currently, she leads a ministry and a business. The ministry is Women of Valour Ministries to help women walk out of the prison cells by understanding their identity in Christ.

The business is Strategic Choice Leadership to help the families, educators, and communities build relationships with the youth.

She accomplishes this through her own transparency and revealing her own masks. She is the loving wife of Carlton L. Monroe and resides in Shrewsbury, PA.

Contact info: andreaemonroe.com.

Her mantra is: God loves you more than your finite mind can ever comprehend.

CHAPTER 33

The Healing Intercessor

After I agreed to become a part of the collaboration, I started to listen to others pray. As I listened to how they prayed, and what they said, I became intimidated. I told myself and the enemy of my soul, "I am NOT an intercessor." I bought into the lie. One day, I came to realize that I am an intercessor, but just a different kind. One I had NEVER heard of before.

My first question was: What is an intercessor? I knew the word "intercessor" from being around and in the church, but I had never looked it up prior to writing this chapter. We can "hear" words and not know what they mean but based on its usage we come up with a meaning.

An intercessor simply means prayer on behalf of another, and naturally arises from the instinct of the human heart – not merely prompted by affection and interest but recognizing that God'srelation to man is not merely individual, but social. (Biblestudytools.com)

What does an intercessor do? What is their role?

· An intercessor's role is to pray when he/she sees or hears a need.

· An intercessor prays for someone who comes to his/her heart/mind or presence.

· An intercessor stands in the gap for the person(s) whom the Holy Spirit brings to his/her attention.

· An intercessor prays for God's divine intervention.

I am learning the heart of God is intercession to reach HIS people. This is one reason we have the church for fellowship. We are called to build up and intercede for each other in and out of the church.

How do I know this? God had intercessors such as Moses and the priests. Then finally, Jesus became Our Ultimate Intercessor according to Hebrews 7:25 AMP:

"Therefore, HE (Christ) is able also to save forever (completely, perfectly, for eternity) those who come to God through HIM since HE always lives to INTERCEDE and INTERVENE on their behalf [with God]."

As I was studying the topic of intercession, I found out that the Holy Spirit is also an intercessor for us according to Romans 8: 26-28. As I read the verses, verse twenty-eight became so clear:

"And we know that God causes ALL things to work together for good for those who are called according to HIS plan and purpose."

Suddenly, the light bulb went off! How is it possible for ALL things to work together for the good?

Because God uses us (through Jesus) to serve as little intercessors to perform HIS will and call on the earth.

On Thanksgiving Day 2021, I was driving to NC to visit family and saw an accident. I immediately began to pray. I often do that when I see an accident. I immediately started praying for healing and salvation for all who were involved in the car accident. I pray that God would lead them or send someone to share information about the saving knowledge of Jesus Christ. After I prayed, the Holy Spirit downloaded to me the words "healing intercessor." I had never heard those words together. I had been saying, "I am NOT an intercessor," but I was asking God to help me compose this chapter or I was going to donate the money to the book project. Every other day, I was trying to back out of writing this chapter.

I recall once, my husband and I were traveling. We were engaged in an enjoyable conversation, and we passed an accident. He literally stopped the conversation mid-sentence and said to me: "Aren't you going topray, we just passed an accident?" I said, "Oh yeah." I began to pray. When I finished, my husband said to me, "Since I have known you, you have ALWAYS prayed for the people involved in accidents."

As I wrote this last paragraph, the Lord just confirmed to me that I am an intercessor for healing.

The Lord started reminding me of times the Healing Intercessor has shown up in my life. I remember finally deciding to go back to my church in person, and I was greeted by an old friend (in the lobby) between services. I hugged him, and he told me that his back was hurting something terrible. I said to him, "The devil is a liar (one of my favorite phrases)! Let us pray." I prayed for his healing. I remember being on a Zoom call with my T-Shirt designer and she said: "My back is hurting." I said, "Lay your hand on your back and we are going to pray." I began to pray for her healing. We had our meeting and I kept it moving. It is not my business to heal, but to intercede through prayer. It is God's business to heal.

It just hit me! I have to laugh at myself, because I do not ask "if I can pray," I tell them. I would say either: "to lay your hand on the area of sickness/pain" or I would ask if I can. And then I ask God to heal and to manifest His presence in that area within that day.

I now know that I am an intercessor. I have the gift of healing. The Holy Spirit has shown me that the way I intercede is tied to my gift. God has wired each one of us so specifically and uniquely.

Take a moment and find out how you too may be an intercessor. It is the very thing that touches your heart. Here are some examples:

· Sex Trafficking

· Homeless

· Domestic Violence

· Parents

· Teachers

· Police officers

· Teens

· Pastors

· Leadership

· Government

It is a burden that is laid upon your heart, by the Lord, to pray. Many times, you may not even realize, like I did not think that it was 'a thing.' BUT it is most definitely 'a thing' that has been given to you. I close with a challenge: Ask God and the people in your circle, "What is it that you pray for the most outside of yourself?"

About the Intercessor

Minister Monica Leak

Monica Leak uses the power of information to reach others through creative content in preached, written, and spoken words. Monica's works include contributions to six Lent devotionals, two women's empowerment anthologies and three self-published collections of social justice themed poetry as well as one collaborative social justice project.

By training she is a speech-language pathologist in southern Maryland and works as an academic librarian at the John Leland Center for Theological Studies. She is a licensed minister and serves as an associate minister at First Baptist Church Vienna in Virginia. You can learn more about Monica by following MLeakPoetry on all social media platforms (Facebook/Instagram/Twitter) and visiting monicaspeaks.org.

CHAPTER 34

Strategies to Take the City

"If you **fail** to **plan**, you are **planning to fail**," is a quote that has circulated in conversation, in articles, books and dialogues for years and now is making the rounds in memes, blogs and posts on the internet. Who can be rightly credited for saying it is controversial as some argue that it is Benjamin Franklin, others Winston Churchill. A similar statement was made in 1973 by televangelist Robert H. Schuller, "Most people fail, not because they lack talent, money, or opportunity; they fail because they never really planned to succeed." Whether said by Franklin, one of the drafters of the Declaration of Independence and the U.S. Constitution and negotiator of the Treaty of Paris or by Churchill the prime minister of the United Kingdom known for his wartime leadership or even the televangelist in a Sunday morning sermon the emphasis is on that of having a plan. This idea of having a plan has applications to all areas of life not just in the natural but also in the spiritual. If God himself has a plan for you according to Jeremiah 29:11(NRSV), "For surely I know the plans I have for you, says the Lord, plans for your welfare and not for harm, to give you a future with hope," then we would do well to have a plan in place to initiate and complete the assignment given to our charge.

The assignment is clear according to Matthew 28:19-20 (NRSV), "**Go** therefore and make disciples of all nations, baptizing them in the name of the Father and of the Son and of the Holy Spirit, and teaching them to obey everything that I have commanded you. And remember, I am with you always, to the end of the age." In other words, we are commissioned to take the cities for the kingdom of God. If we are going to be effective in carrying out that assignment then there must be a plan, a strategy. What is strategy? Strategy is defined as, "a plan, method, or series of maneuvers or stratagems for obtaining a specific goal or result:" To initiate and complete the assignment given we must have a strategy. To take our cities for the kingdom of God, I offer three strategies for your consideration: 1. Set your targets 2. Prepare the plan and finally 3. Mobilize and employ your resources in the natural and in the spiritual realm.

To set the targets as intercessors we need to have an accurate knowledge of the enemy, knowledge of the principalities over our cities, the conditions of our cities and in a step ahead have the prophetic foresight praying into the future. 1 Peter 5:8 says, "Discipline yourselves, keep alert. Like a roaring lion your adversary the devil prowls around, looking for someone to devour." Since we know the enemy is on the loose then it is important as intercessors that we take our position to make up the hedge and stand before the Lord according to Ezekiel 22:30 and to position ourselves upon our watch post according to Habakkuk 2:1. Knowing our enemy also requires us knowing some of his tactics and strategies such as rejection, anger, low self-esteem, pride, addiction, shame, fear, jealousy, infirmity, and control. These attacks when launched may manifest in feelings of tiredness, depression, lack of energy, isolation, acting out verbally, even acting out of character. As intercessors we are on our watch so we can see what is coming, all are properly equipped, trained and in a state of readiness according to (Ephesians 6:1-11). Bill Bright, founder of Campus Crusade and Loren Cunningham, founder of Youth With a Mission (YWAM), "concluded that in order to truly transform any nation with the Gospel of Jesus Christ, these seven facets of society must be reached: Religion, Family, Education, Government, Media, Arts & Entertainment and Business."

From those seven targets you develop a plan in alignment with the will of God. Proverbs 19:21 (NKJV) says "There are many plans in a man's heart, Nevertheless the Lord's counsel—that will stand." Inquire of the Lord the plans and give yourself to prayer and He will answer with next steps. The plan includes position whether it is that of the five-fold as outlined in Ephesians 4:11-12 or the exercising of the gifts of the spirit by the body according to 1 Corinthians 12:7-11. Regardless of position and title Your position allows you to see what is coming, prepare, anticipate the advancement of the enemy afar off. Be mindful that your steps have been ordered by the Lord. He knows the way that you take

Having the plan in place it is time to mobilize. We move into position according to Matthew 29: 19, " Go ye therefore, and teach all nations, baptizing them in the name of the Father, and of the Son, and of the Holy Ghost:" We stand ready fully equipped to pull down strongholds and cast down imaginations that are causing havoc in our cities

(2Crinthians 10:3-5), While you may have a different position in the body we are all members working toward the same goal of taking our cities for the kingdom of God.

Men and women of God we have been called to intercede in such a time as this, to make up the hedge. We can take the city by setting our targets, making a plan, and mobilizing into the hedges and highways to compel people to come into the kingdom.

Prayer Declaration: I decree that I have been called for this time to intercede so that the kingdom of this world becomes the kingdom of our Lord. (Revelation 11:15).

About the Intercessor

Elder Ivy Caldwell

Ivy Caldwell is the Founder of Footprint Enterprises, LLC which is a faith-based organization located in Rochester, NY which serves those who are ready to confront their past or present emotional trauma head on from domestic abuse, sexual abuse, relationship abuse or low self-esteem and be healed through her Signature Coaching Program "Stepping Into ANEW You." She will coach you through the process by implementing strategies with her step-by-step system. If you are ready to move forward with your life, to get your voice and authority back you can contact her through her website https://footprintenterprisesllc.com

She is an ordained elder, wife, mother, author, course creator, international speaker and a certified life coach and Christian counselor. She is the author of "Expose It" which is her personal testimony of overcoming childhood abuse. Collaborations consist of "Speak Up...We Deserve to Be Heard" and "Walking In My Purpose."

Go ahead and expose your truth so you can be healed.

CHAPTER 35

When the Attacks Begin

Get ready, get ready and I mean get ready for the attacks to come because they will surely come. When you are a Christian of course the attacks are going to come but because you are an intercessor the attacks will be elevated to a higher level. Do not you think for one moment that your adversary is going to sit idly by while you are working for God and tearing his kingdom down. The enemy will send thorns, boomerangs, fiery darts, assaults, and missiles.

What are those **thorns**? A thorn is something that will nag at you. You can go about your day to day and your life but there is something nagging at you physically, mentally, or emotionally. Physically there will be pain in your body, and you are believing God to heal you. You have been praying for others to be healed. Your healing has not manifested yet and you become discouraged. Paul had a thorn in his flesh that he desired God to move but God told him my grace is sufficient for thee. The same goes for us as we continue to believe God no matter what we may feel. "And He said to me, *My grace is* sufficient for you, for *My* strength *is* made perfect in weakness. Therefore, most gladly *I* will rather boast in *my* infirmities, that the power of Christ may rest upon me." (II Corinthians 12:9) Who goes around boasting in our infirmities?

We go around murmuring, complaining, and amplifying the thorn instead of magnifying God's Word. God's grace is sufficient for each one of us. God's power is resting upon you. We continue to look unto God the author and finisher of our faith and wait on Him to move on our behalf.

What is a **boomerang**? "For God is not mocked, whatsoever a man soweth, that he will also reap." Have you ever hurt anyone in your life? Sure, we all have but when it happens to us, we take on the attitude of how dare they do or say this about me. We are shocked that they did it. Have you ever looked at a boomerang as something that I did to someone at some point in my life? Now it has happened to me, but it is even worse.

So do not be so quick to get upset. Think of it as your boomerang for what you have sown, and this is your harvest. Have you ever said that will never be me? Keep living! God has a way of making us eat our own words. Boomerangs also teach us not to be so quick to judge others.

What are those **fiery darts**? A fiery dart is an underhanded jab at you. It hurts you to your core. Usually those that are closest to us throw the fiery darts when they want to get to us. It could be intentional or not. It's something that we have not dealt with yet. Why does it sting? We are not supposed to be quick to offense, right?

"Woe to the world because of offenses! For offenses must come, but woe to that man by whom the *offense* comes!" (Matthew 18:7) Offenses will come but for some reason we are thrown aback because of them. "We give no *offense* in anything, that our ministry may not be blamed." (II Corinthians 6:3). No matter what happens to us we are not to give offense in anything because we are ambassadors for Christ. Yes, it hurts, and you cannot believe they said that to you. They are supposed to love you and they said that to you. I encourage you to deal with that issue until it is no longer a fiery dart. Think it not strange when the fiery darts come. "above all, taking the shield of faith with which, you will be able to quench all the *fiery* darts of the wicked one." (Ephesians 6:16) We are admonished to quench all the fiery darts that come our way.

What do you do when the **assaults** come? I have experienced an assault on my character and my name. I spoke the truth and nothing but the truth. I was accused of not doing something before and I know I did it. I did not say one word to defend myself. I know who I am and whose I am. I am a woman of God, a child of God, His friend, His prophet, His servant, and His mouthpiece. Most of all I am God's intercessor and God honors me as I honor Him. God watches over His word to perform it. When I use God's word in prayer it is a guarantee, and it will come to pass because I believe God will do it. I do not worry about the naysayers because I know what God's Word says, "Touch not mine anointed and do my prophets no harm." Whenever someone harmed or touched someone who belonged to God in the Bible their end was not good at all. That is why I can pray for my enemies because they do not know who I am and what they are doing. They are doing themselves harm.

What are **missiles**? A missile brings life altering destruction with it. The aftermath of the destruction is so devastating you wonder how you will pick up the fragmented pieces. There seems to be no hope and you want to give up but something on the inside of you says, "No"! You cannot give up and you must keep fighting this thing called life. Whenever I experience a setback in life no matter what it is I know that God allowed it to happen to me and there must be a purpose for it. With God we can stand against the attacks of the enemy because we are girded up in the Word and prayer. One thing about God: He works best with fragmented pieces.

Scriptures taken from NKJV

About the Intercessor

Prophetess Marie-Claude Clement

Prophetess Marie-Claude Clement is an anointed Woman of God committed to evoking change *(within)* the body of Christ by equipping, encouraging, strengthening, and praying the Word of God. As the CEO of Inspirational Life and Business Coaching, she is an advocate for domestic violence and mental health in the church.

CHAPTER 36

The Refined Intercessor

When I first met Dr. Monique Rogers on the Clubhouse app, I never expected her to ask me to participate in a book collaboration with other authors. Being a person who struggles with saying, "No," I immediately answered, "Yes" however, deep down inside I really wanted to say, "No." At first thought, I could not believe that God called me to work on this project with so many women whom I've never walked a day in their shoes. Most of these women are walking in their purpose, with their own businesses, and have written books before this project and are well known in their respective industry. Here I stand having achieved none of those things or titles until this very moment.

As a Haitian descent, English is not my first language and I have always struggled with writing essay papers at school. Let us just say my writing was so horrible, that the other students made fun of me and called me all types of names like (stupid, dummy, illiterate, and retard). The teacher as well did not make it easy for me, because I was the only student who had the reddest marks for grammatical errors on all my essays. Therefore, the thought of being an author was so far away from my mind. Why was God asking me to face my fears of writing now? This was the one time I wished I could be like Elijah in the bible and go hide in a cave and only come out once this nightmare was over.

That night, I could not wait to go into the presence of God and speak to him concerning the very notion of facing my fears of writing. Like Joseph, I wrestled with God and told him all the reasons why I did not qualify for this job. I reminded him of my struggles with English grammar and all the names I was called by students. I also made it my business to remind him how I stayed up crying all night and dreaded going to school because I was so embarrassed as if God did not know any of these things. After all, he witnessed the tears and saw me through the pain and heartache. Who was I to argue and fight with God? My mother always had a saying I am not sure where she got it from but it went like this, "Your arm is too short to box with God," meaning, "You cannot outwit God." This I remember while attempting to battle knowing on the inside that I was eventually going to lose this battle. After presenting my case and acknowledging that I had lost, I decided to surrender and told God to have his way.

The next morning, at around 3: 00 AM, I was awakened by God. I knew this was him because this is normally the time God speaks to me. Like a child yearning to hear her father's voice, my ears were attuned, and I welcomed my daddy to speak. God first ensured his love for me and told me not to be afraid, because he chose me and not man. He reminded me that man looks at the outer appearance, however he looks at the heart and I am the perfect person to carry out this project and write the book. After hearing God, I told him to have his way and I reminded myself of this scripture: Philippians 4:13 (Amplified Version)

"I can do all things [which He has called me to do] through Him who strengthens and empowers me [to fulfill His purpose—I am self-sufficient in Christ's sufficiency; I am ready for anything and equal to anything through Him who infuses me with inner strength and confident peace."

Before the Spirit of God left, I heard him say very faintly "You are my Refined Intercessor." I did not know what that meant however, I now knew the chapter title for my portion of the book.

I could not wait to tell Dr. Rogers my topic, I was so excited and knew confidently that indeed I am the right person. At 10:00 AM, I called Dr. Rogers and told her my chapter topic. She was so excited that she asked me permission to use the refined intercessor name for her next conference. Wow! Here I was trying to ditch out of this assignment and did not know that I was the answer to someone else's prayer. God always surprises me and all the time I am humble. What more could I say except for, "Let's get the writing done, Marie-Claude"!

So, what is a "Refined Intercessor"?

In the Bible God references the word refined as purifying from what is gross, coarse, vulgar, inelegant, low, and the like; to make elegant or excellent; to polish; as, to refine the manners, the language, the style, the taste, the intellect, or the moral feelings. An intercessor can be defined as a person who by calling or by nature chooses to be a mediator on behalf of those who cannot intervene for themselves. Therefore, a "Refined Intercessor," exemplifies these characteristics:

1. God-focused, God-Confident, and not self-focused or confident in self solely

2. Willing to sacrifice self and allow God to take them through his fire to take everything out of their life that is not like him

3. One that allows the heart of God to flow through them no matter how they feel

4. One that hungers and thirsts after righteousness and holiness through their intercession

5. Understands the importance of the fear and reverence of God and guards their hearts, mind, and body from sin and disobedience

6. One that desires and is willing to see God's promises fulfilled in another person's life, nation, or world, even though your own life looks dark and dry.

If you were able to identify with any of the above, congratulations, you are God's, "Refined Intercessor." Keep pressing behind the veil!

About the Intercessor

Christine Ugbomah

Christine immigrated to the United States at an early age from the UK .and comes from a large family who is very into music and entertainment. She is a plural artist, poet, and author. Christine has self-published several books on Kindle and Amazon. Her passion is to lead, encourage and motivate women she has been called to uplift by faith through her devotional journals and workbooks. Christine spends her time learning new techniques in the arts. Her work has been showcased in places such as The Carnegie Museum for Art for her artwork in Photography: The August Wilson African American Cultural Center for her art and jewelry making techniques. Christine's powdered glass work was displayed in the Pittsburgh Glass Center Gallery. Christine is always in school and is currently working on her bachelor's with hopes of becoming an art therapist soon, and her favorite color is blue.

CHAPTER 37

The Art of Prayer

Prayer is like a well-layered portrait or a beautiful, sculptured work of art. The process of chipping away from cold slabbed marble or an endless layer of oil paint takes up to three weeks to dry from the inside out. Prayer is like a piece of art that you must take time to work on; it simply cannot be your piece if you do not plan the finished look of it from the beginning and commit to long hours and weeks to see the finished work. Here we see that faith reaches the piece long before it is started. By faith, we enter prayer knowing the outcome is assured.

So is the art of prayer. It is a process that takes time and a layer of commitment to break through the forces of darkness, impeding the carefully carved out purpose and plan of a loving father. When God gave us prayer as a weapon, he also gave us a blank Canvas and, our words are the brushes that paint and the pen of a ready writer to sketch out the details we clearly access from the tools prayer needs, which is faith, endurance, a position of righteous and a heart that contains no offense or unforgiveness. These requirements are critical long before we intercede in the lives of those we are called to pray for!

A father who has left no stone unturned to ensure that His vessels carry out His master plan of bringing back to Him His precious children, as well as the process of breaking through any hidden thing or agenda that comes to block and hinder the promises of God to manifest in their lives. It is the art of prayer that breaks every yoke, plot, and method of an enemy who relentlessly tries to stop our prayer lives with anything he deems will take away our focus during our times of intercession.

As we stand in the gap as yielded vessels of honor to break chains and bondages through willing hearts and minds, we are fearless in viewing the future successes that can only become a reality through prayer. Targeted prayer that goes beyond the natural punctures the supernatural realms of time and space.

Victory is guaranteed; as we engage in thoughts of success in the premise of our stammering lips, we shall See victory from the knee-bending position we occupy. We must come with faith or not at all because there are times that we are praying for others in secret. There must be a strong belief system that the promise of victory given to us through His word will be manifested in the earth! We must earnestly press into the very things God is showing us in order to carry out God's plan as he uses us to intercede on behalf of others.

One thing about prayer is that there is no distance that prayer cannot reach, counteract, or add to any one person, place or anything that is needed. When we are called to pray, we are given an opportunity to bring change solutions and even information that would not come any other way but through prayer, if this is the way God is wooing us to get a strategy along the way.

Simply put, prayer is talking to God about situations, journeys, issues, and much-valued assignments given out to people to advance the kingdom. God has given us the assignment to take up arms in prayer as we fight offensively in prayer.

Once we begin to. See the manifested glory of our continuous prayer points emerging in the earth; it is fantastic and fulfilling to see the answered prayers Creating an image of life and exhaling breaths as we enjoy the very fruit of a commitment to stand in the gap or for someone else and even for ourselves. Earnest Prayer assignments showed me strategically (there had been no one for years who would walk alongside me in prayer, which made me the artist of one canvas and no one to collaborate on the piece at hand). So, I practiced this art until victory arrived. Beloved, so shall it happen for you! Stand your ground and stay on the wall until that prayer has been answered. Stay until you change long before the answer has shown up. Because you cannot use the art of prayer and stay the same. It is impossible to even stay at the same level of faith. It is impossible to remain in the realms of prayer and not shift. Today I encourage you not to despise your circumstances; they are God ordained to bring you through triumphantly.

A Prayer

Heavenly Father, I pray that you will draw those who read these words into a place of prayer that will release a sweet aroma like an expensive perfume that lingers long after its use, and that their prayer is guided higher and higher, reaching your throne awaiting your sovereign answer. An answer that by faith has manifested because of their unwavering faith in you.

In Jesus' name Amen.

About the Intercessor

Pastor Darlene Thorne

Darlene Thorne, MDiv, is the CEO of A Heart After the Father, LLC and serves as your Caregiver's Coach/Mentor. Her mission is to influence change to women ministry leaders teaching them how to practice positive, intentional personal self-care, body, soul and spirit.

As an International speaker, Darlene delivers a life-impacting message. Featured on television and radio, Darlene focuses on walking in total freedom and authenticity.

As an Amazon number one best selling author, Pastor Darlene has written several books and participated in over five anthologies. Each of her books are written to encourage a deeper relationship with God and foster time in the presence of Abba.

She and her husband Kevin, Sr. serve together as pastors at Renewal Community Church in Clayton, NC. They have two world changer young adults, Kevin, II and Kennedy Elayne. You may contact Darlene Thorne at https://linktr.ee/Ladydarlene

CHAPTER 38

Abba, May I Represent You Well

By Pastor Darlene Thorne

As we approach the throne of our Father, we may want to do some self-examination. Yes, God does want us to come to Him just as we are - but there are some things we may want to consider as we are coming into His presence. It is not enough to come in and just start talking like we talk to our friend. God wants us to be honest and commune with Him, however, He is also to be reverenced. Our parents want us to be honest with them and to share the truth with them, however, we are also to remember they are our parents. We do not call them by their first name and just talk. We show a level of respect for them because of who they are. We are to do the same when we come before the Father's throne. This puts us in position to truly hear from heaven.

How much do we desire to hear from the Lord? How much do we desire to know the deep things of God? To answer these questions, we must make it our business to approach Abba with the knowledge of His will for those we will be interceding for. Not that God will give us the blueprint, but He will lead us to the word and with the scriptures we are to pray over those He lays on our hearts. So how we come before the Lord is so important. We want to have clean hands and a pure heart before Him. We want to see miracles performed, we want to know and hear about the miraculous things that need to happen for His glory. In order for this to take place, we must be in position to understand how to pray.

First, we must know the word and what God says about a thing or situation, etc.,

*Pray the word

*Study the word

*Soak in His presence

*Listen for His voice

*Speak God's word

*Live as though it is already done

*Be a vessel of honor

*Live, live, live our life to please Him

Secondly, make fasting a regular part of your life. When you fast, you do several things:

1. You allow your natural body to rest and recalibrate;

2. You allow your focus to be on prayer and the word;

3. Your heart is turned toward God and what He wants to lay on your heart; 4. You have a heightened sensitivity to Holy Spirit and how He desires to move in and through you.

I have found that in my time of intercession, my heart becomes softened to the things of the Spirit. Not only that, I see the body of Christ in a new way. One thing I recall asking the Lord for was the ability to see people through His eyes. I want my heart to break with the things that have broken His heart. When we pray for others, we take the focus off of us and our own issues. One thing I have experienced is the change that takes place in my heart. As I am praying at times I begin to weep and at times I do not know why but I then I will begin to pray in the Holy Ghost. As I pray as I call it the "perfect prayer," I pray until I receive a release in my spirit that the burden is lifted. That can be minutes or longer depending on what is happening in the spirit realm. There again is where we must be sensitive to the Spirit of God. When the release comes then we are free to go on to pray for the next thing or then wait in the presence of Abba for Him to speak to our hearts.

I read a book called The Art of Intercession by Rees Howell and it chronicles his life as an intercessor. In this book, we follow his journey of getting a burden to pray for not only people but for nations. We read of the time he spends in prayer, sometimes minutes, other times hours are spent in travail for a country. This man influenced the lives of so many people! His heart for prayer was amazing. He would fast and pray and hold prayer vigils that lasted at times for days. He would not eat because he would have such a burden for something God laid on his heart. He lived by the premise that he wanted to be the one God would call for to stand in the gap to bring victory to a nation. As I read that book, it caused me to want to have that same desire for the Lord to use me to impact others. What a privilege it is to be called upon to be the warrior in prayer to bring change to a situation!

About the Intercessor

Prophetess Renee Brown

Renee Brown is an ordained Prophetess from Minneapolis, MN, she graduated with an Associate and Bachelor's Degree in Social Work-attached with marriage counseling and Early learning childhood, known in pursuit of her Doctorate Degree.

Entrepreneur anointing of MorningStar Cleaning Service, Love-and Learn Daycare and her new business, Begin In Good Health.

Renee is now serving under a strong Apostolic and Prophetic Leadership of Apostle John Eckhardt, who is the overseer of

Crusader Ministries located in Chicago, Illinois.

Renee is called to impart and activate the gifts of the spirit through prayer, teaching, and deliverance. She is trained and trains other in the prophetic school of Ministering the Spiritual Gifts assistant to

Prophet Karen Guice head of the Prophet and Prophetic ministry under Apostle John Eckhardt

Renee has also ministered in the song of the Lord as a psalmist on the prophetic praise and worship team with Prophetess Kathy Summers, under Apostle John Eckhardt.

Prophetess Renee is dedicated to the perfecting of the saints for the work of the ministry with a strong prophetic teaching under apostolic grace.

Renee has also Assisted Pat Garnes in Crusaders Church as an assistant administrator in new members' class & helps of Ministry class.

Renee's desire is to help God's saints fully recognize their place within the kingdom of God and marketplace through prayer and the teaching of the prophetic word of the Lord, by way of the Holy Spirit of God to fulfill the call of God on their lives. Renee has a loving relationship with her Family in Chicago IL, Mother Rachelle, daughter Brittney, grandson, Rodney, and granddaughter, Chosen Channel Collins, and Rosemary & Christopher Brown.

CHAPTER 39

Spiritual Warfare in the Push...

Are you up against unseen forces occupying a seat of authority where you have not gotten that breakthrough in your intercession, and you must keep pushing and pushing through the spiritual realm? No matter what seat of authority and resistance your face in this battle alone Do not stop, I am reminded of the word of the lord from Jacob "And he said, I will not let thee go, except thou bless me. If your reading this book at this time, it is your set time of breakthrough.

Genesis 32:26, KJV

"I can do all things through Christ which strengtheneth me."

Philippians 4:13 KJV

"For our struggle is not against flesh and blood [contending only with physical opponents], but against the rulers, against the powers, against the world forces of this [present] darkness, against them spiritual forces of wickedness in the heavenly (supernatural) places."

Ephesians 6:12 AMP

"I want to encourage you, Don't You give up, Don't you lose heart you can do this, you have what it takes to get your breakthrough, So Don't Stop praying, worshipping, studying and speaking the word of God."

Romans 4:17 KJV

"God, who quickeneth the dead, and calleth those things which be not as though they were."

Keep persevering in (PRAYER), continuing firmly or obstinately in a course of action, in spite of difficulty or opposition, as you keep taking your spiritual authority in the spiritual realm, remember that it is your responsibility for your life. Do not depend on everyone else for your spiritual well-being and spiritual breakthroughs. Why? Because greater is he that is on the inside of you then he that is in the world He will open the eyes of your understanding and give you wisdom with strategic moves.

The Parable on Prayer

Now Jesus was telling the disciples a parable to make the point that at all times they ought to pray and not give up and lose heart, saying, "In a certain city there was a judge who did not fear God and had no respect for man. There was a [desperate] widow in that city and she kept coming to him and saying, 'Give me justice (avenge) and legal protection from my adversary.' For a time, he would not; but later he said to himself, 'Even though I do not fear God nor respect man, yet because this widow continues to bother me, I will give her justice and legal protection; otherwise by continually coming she [will be an intolerable annoyance and she] will wear me out.'" Then the Lord said, "Listen to what the unjust judge says! And will not [our just] God defend and avenge His elect [His chosen ones] who cry out to Him day and night? Will He delay [in providing justice] on their behalf? I tell you that He will defend and avenge them quickly.

However, when the Son of Man comes, will He find [this kind of persistent] faith on the earth? Luke 18:8 AMP

Proverbs 4:23 AMP

"Watch over your heart with all diligence, For from it flow the springs of life."

Please, let me help you out here, what we just read was spoken from the mouth of Jesus as it is written in red. He has just given us a word of wisdom and encouragement, and the widow woman has just shown us her desperate, persistent cry in an unfavorable plea with Human resistance and Satanic delays. The widow woman's pushing, and persistence disturbed the unjust judge, who fears not the Lord nor men. Hear this, her pushing in caused him to receive a revelation of our God, and how she was the chosen one, and her God would not delay in defending or avenge her quickly. Our Father is looking for your faith in this earth realm

Please hear what the spirit of the Lord is saying to you today. In my closing let us decree and declare right know that every spirit of heartbreak, discouragement, defeat, doubt, fear, and prayerlessness (because you are not seeing the microwave results) be broken off you now In Jesus' Name, and that the Power of the Holy Spirit and the Zeal of the Lord will arise on the inside of you to breakthrough every spirit of heaviness and resistance, I Decree you shall breakthrough with great victory. You shall receive the stamina to stand your ground and, after you have done everything, to stand!

Exodus 14:13-14 KJV

"And Moses said unto the people, Fear ye not, stand still, and see the salvation of the LORD, which he will shew to you today: for the Egyptians whom ye have seen today, ye shall see them again no more forever. The LORD shall fight for you, and ye shall hold your peace."

About The Intercessor

Marie Brown

Marie Brown is an experienced professional in the field of accounting, external auditing, and quality assurance audit with a history of working in private and Government organizations. She is also a freelance accountant, consultant, and registered student mentor where she provides mentorship to tertiary individuals.

Marie Brown holds designation as Chartered Certified Accountant (ACCA), FCCA and a master's degree in professional accounting with the University of London. She is passionate about giving back to the community and is a member of the Kiwanis Club of West St.

Andrew and a co-founder of the Tamaike and Marie Brown Foundation, established in January 2021 at the Marymount High School in Jamaica for students who are performing excellently in their academic and other curriculum activities. Marie is a newly published Co- Author in the book titled Called To Intercede.

CHAPTER 40

The Power of the Prayer of a Consecrated Submissive Warrior

Prayer and fasting are the connecting forces that open the portal to the throne room of Grace and create that connection with the supreme God. Throughout the Bible we see where prayer and fasting from consecrated vessels brings forth miracles, signs, and wonders. They both bring persons into the right alignment, expectancy, and faith.

As a child growing up, I never understood the reason my grandfather wanted us to pray when we woke up, before eating, and before going to bed every day, even when we were reluctant to do so. With my limited understanding at that time, we were cheated of leisure time and rest. I thought that he was too stringent on us. However, years later I realized that these times of prayer were laying the foundation for deeper intimacy and a greater relationship with God. They were also a deposit into our future and for generations to come.

This principle became a norm from childhood through adulthood. The connection deepens to the extent where I speak to God first about everything. A place where God revealed to me through dreams and visions of things happening, things to come, and warnings about things and situations I should not venture into.

Did I listen to these warnings? No. I allow my flesh to take the prominent position while ignoring the revelation of God. I eventually suffered the consequences, resulting in emotional damages. John 15:4 (Paraphrased) reminds us that we need to abide in the presence of God as we ourselves cannot bear fruit unless we abide in the vine.

Lack of an effective prayer life of an intercessor

Being disobedient while starving your prayer life is very dangerous. It takes you away from the throne room of God and will open you up to different attacks from the enemy. The once consecrated vessel is now occupied with things not of God. Growing up in an environment where prayer was an integral process of our day to day lives, I was once in a place where I gave up on God because He was not moving as fast as I wanted Him to, I saw wrong being done but there was no justice. The questions were where is God? Why does He allow these things to happen? This led to frustration and disobedience.

This state was a dangerous place to be, this is where the enemy has the legal right to enter in and do as he pleases. Satan does not care about us; all he wants is to destroy our future by chaining us to circumstances and situations, preventing us from walking into our God given purpose. Disobedience towards God can open the door to strongholds such as unforgiveness, bitterness, depression, spirit of heaviness, etc. A place where the gifting is prominent, but the Fruit of the Spirit is not evident, while exposing your family members and those around you to attack from the enemy.

But our God is faithful and true when we confess our sins, He will forgive us and purify us from all unrighteousness (John 1:9). He will send the right person to help walk with you through your healing.

Being complacent and lackadaisical will not help, it takes repentance, submission to God and His words, confessions, and the willingness to go back to your first Love.

The power of a praying intercessor

The prayer of a consecrated intercessor can shift times and seasons, bringing to the natural realm what God has released in the spiritual realm. A consecrated intercessor's prayers can release complete healing, deliverance, restoration etc. An intercessor should never proclaim to be without sin as you deceive yourself (1John 1:8) but should never be a stranger to prayer, fasting, reading, meditating on the word of God, and forgiveness.

Through intercession, while in a place of obedience, I saw where family members who were unsaved got saved, persons whom I prayed for individually and collectively, were healed. Situations that seemed difficult became easy. Therefore, there is no doubt in my mind that Intercession works. I also see other intercessors praying for others, situations, and things, receiving God's response.

Being obedient and remaining consistent in your prayer life helps to develop a strong relationship with God and improve your prayer life. You will also position yourself to receive strategies from God on how to pray, what to pray for, and how to pray against things before it enters the atmosphere. You will be equipped to come against anything that seeks to attack you.

Conclusion

It is very important that, as gatekeepers, we ensure we consistently maintain a posture of forgiveness and purification. Cleansing our temple every day and allowing the Holy spirit to take control of our mind, body, soul, and spirit. When we pray for ourselves, our family, or others through the will of God, we will not just be impactful, but invoke God's presence into our atmosphere and whatever we are praying about. This will also prevent us from being exposed to uncharted territory, or attacks that would have been avoided if we were in the will of God.

About the Intercessor

Meri Horton

Meri Horton is a Certified Premarital/Marital Coach. Meri is also a co-founder of Mission Possible Institute. This non-profit organization provides families (the way) to a strong community by providing coaching sessions, customized workshops, training sessions and events to strengthen the community. Moreover, she is exciting, interesting, imaginative, while using commonsense with her direct humorous personality. Meri offers God's word, woven with individual experiences, to draw in lives with adaptability and change.

Meri Horton serves as an elder at Destined To Win Christian Center. She has been married for over 29 years. She and her husband are still romantically in love with each other. They are the proud parents of three children and two grandchildren.

CHAPTER 41

The Power of Intercession in Marriage
The Power of Intercession in Marriage: A Husband's Perspective

As the husband, I was living a lie, but present every time the church doors opened no matter rain or sunshine. I worked in the ministry faithfully, and tonight was no different. Every Wednesday night is dedicated to Bible Study, and I vividly remember this Wednesday and have never forgotten the memories of this night. On this unforgettable Wednesday night, I was in my bedroom watching pornography and heard my wife open the door. I quickly removed the video tape out of the VCR and hid it in my drawer. I greeted my wife and kids as if nothing was wrong and without conviction because I was addicted. A few moments later, I hastily left for Bible Study. To my surprise, my wife and kids stayed home. When I arrived at church, the secretary ran to me saying, "Your wife is on the phone." I never imagined what would happen next. I said, "Hello," and my wife was screaming so loud I could barely understand what she was saying, until I heard her say, "I found the porn tapes and the stash of adult magazines."

At that moment, all I could think about was, "How much does she know?" Honestly, I wasn't worried about my marriage, my children, nor my relationship with God, "I WAS CAUGHT!"

I was selfish! I did not think about the impact it would have on everyone involved or my future. The days ahead were hard, but one of the men at the church offered mentorship. He prayed with me, and we would read the word together. This was exactly what I needed: prayer, accountability, and hope.

Each passing day, I looked at my wife and girls and saw the pain in their eyes. My prayer was to be the best husband and father that I could be from this moment forward. I only knew one way to be delivered. I began to cry out to God! I stayed on my knees and cried out for the mercy of God. No, I did not complete a 12-step program, but I do now understand the power of a confessing addict.

An addict is only one look or thought away from relapse. I have to pray and kill my flesh daily so that the addiction does not win. My advice to any addict is to ask God to reveal to you the root of the problem. The bible talks about being drawn away, by your own lust and enticed, in James 1. So, when it comes to porn addiction, do not try to hide it, confess it to God first and to any others affected by your actions for forgiveness and complete healing. The bible reminds us to flee from sin. I learned that it was not worth it. I let down God, my wife, my family, and myself. Getting out of this was not easy, but God in his grace and mercy brought me through this and he can do the same for you. Intercession is very important and needed. God does not want us to bear our burdens alone.

As the wife, I remember it like it was yesterday, that Wednesday was also rainy and gloomy.

I rushed into the house with two young toddlers to prepare for the evening. I decided not to attend Bible Study and stayed home. As I was going about the evening, I went into my husband dresser to put his clothes away and found pornographic videos. I then went looking for what else I could find. In the garage were more videos and adult magazines.

The Power of Intercession in Marriage: A Wife's Perspective

As the wife, I remember it like it was yesterday, that Wednesday was also rainy and gloomy.

I rushed into the house with two young toddlers to prepare for the evening. I decided not to attend Bible Study and stayed home. As I was going about the evening, I went into my husband's dresser to put his clothes away and found pornographic videos. I then went looking for what else I could find. In the garage, I found more videos and adult magazines. Without even thinking, I called the church. As soon as he answered, I went off! I was going to tell the pastor and anyone else that would listen. I wanted my husband to feel the pain and embarrassment.

I asked, "Who is this man?" "Do I even really know him?" These unanswered questions resulted in feelings of insecurity and low self-esteem. I felt not good enough and had experienced the ultimate betrayal. To get back at him, I would constantly be disrespectful, I had lost all respect for him.

I was hurting emotionally, spiritually, and physically. I was in pain! Finally, God sent me a mentor who encouraged and reminded me what the Word says about healing and forgiveness and how to apply it in my marriage. There are times, I slipped back into the old way of thinking. She would patiently direct me back to the word of God. My mentor spent time praying with me, over me, and for my strength. I could not wait to meet with my pastor. I was filled with so much peace on the inside. No one knew what I was going to do or say about our future. I was no longer walking in fear.

On our way to the church, the car was so quiet you could hear a pin drop. When we arrived, the office secretary greeted us. As we walked into Pastor Watson's office, I could hear Worship music from the sanctuary. He greeted us with a hug and a big smile. The office was cozy and warm, and we prayed first. Don't get me wrong it was not a worship service or marriage retreat it was a marriage counseling session, and let's be clear words were exchanged.

I boldly and confidently stated, "I want my marriage! I had a made-up mind. I made a decision to let God be God in this situation. I wanted to be the type of woman who stands by her husband and prays for him in spite of the pain. I began praying the word over my husband and in time I started to see him the way God sees him through Jesus. I began declaring, "LORD, I thank You for my husband. Thank You for creating him in Your image, designing him for greatness and strength. God, please give my husband the joy of

having true wisdom and following good counsel. God, I pray that my husband will seek you daily through prayer, your Word and your voice." I remember the words that came out of Pastor Watson's mouth, "Sis, you have matured, I can tell that prayer has worked." As I walked out of that office, it was a walk of Victory. That day, I was inspired to become the wife that God has called me to be, and I know the importance of seeing my husband through the word of God. God gives us experiences so that we can encourage each other and show what is possible. With God and prayer, all things are possible. This is our story, and we want you to know that Intercession works in Marriages!

About the Intercessor

Kingdom Ambassador Darlene Mingo

Darlene Mingo is the Founder of Talking Kingdom Outreach and is an Award-winning Internet Radio Show host for her former show, Talking Kingdom Live on Facebook. For the last several years she has been a willing vessel that uses her gifts to serve the broken and the homeless.

She was called to the ministry of service when she became saved at the age of thirty. As she was not raised in church like many, she shares her story of how the Holy spirit spoke to her at a red light while in the car. She confesses that the Lord does speak to sinners if they have an ear to hear, a heart to receive and a mind to understand. It is her life's work to help the unchurched to establish a relationship with God for themselves.

CHAPTER 42

When Life Speaks

Most of us have had situations in which we have encountered life experiences that may knock the wind out of our sail. The death of a loved one, loss of a job, divorce, maybe even the disconnection between a parent and a child. Life happens and it comes to teach us, but are we listening?

One of the things that we sometimes fail to understand is when life speaks, God is also speaking. Using life situations to teach us that we cannot handle these circumstances on our own and that God is always near. As life speaks to us to grow us up in God, we sometimes lose our voice because the pain or dismay of what is happening causes us to not know what to say or do and we feel alone. Can you relate?

Our mother went home to be with the Lord, in June of 2016. She had been sick over several years due to lung disease. As a daughter, I took care of my mother during her sickness. We prayed, we fasted, and she became well. I then moved from New Jersey to North Carolina. My mother's sickness began to get worse. My daughters and I traveled back and forth each time she was hospitalized, and I would stay in the hospital room with her. I would play worship music and read the word. There was one occasion in which my brother called and said that our mother was not doing well, and her health was declining rapidly.

We got in our car and hurried back home to New Jersey. As we traveled down the highway, I prayed, cried, and worshiped all the way there. By the time I reached the hospital, she had been moved out of the ICU into a regular room. When we arrived, she was resting. As usual, I stayed in the hospital room, sleeping on the recliner chair. Early that morning her doctor arrived in the room. Amazed, she stated, "Geraldine, you looked NOTHING like this the last time I saw you!" She then turned to me and said, "Whatever magic you have, leave it here." My mother and I both replied, "There is no magic, it is JESUS!!" I am not sure if she pondered exploring a relationship with GOD after witnessing his works, but I can assure you of this, she definitely was a WITNESS.

In Romans 8:34-39, Jesus is interceding on our behalf. Isn't that wonderful to know? Although life experiences happen, and the winds may blow. God will use any willing vessel to intercede when a sister, when a brother, when a family member, when an enemy, when a stranger is unable to open their mouths. What a comfort to know that there is a friend that sticks closer than a brother, and his name is JESUS.

Prayer: Father, we thank you and honor you for your healing. I ask that you touch anyone who is reading this where life has shown up and is attempting to rattle their faith. Holy Spirit, speak to their minds and their hearts. Remind them of GOD'S promises! Remind them that they belong to the Father and, although life happens, it cannot steal what does not belong to it. We rejoice in your word; we rejoice in your presence. We THANK YOU in advance that you are an on time, GOD, and that our life is your GLORY. In Jesus Name. Amen

About the Intercessor

Tara Tate

Tara began her walk with the LORD when she accepted Christ in 1997. Christ called her into a closer walk with him a few years later. She was directed to Calvary Chapel Cary in North Carolina where her foundation in the Word came through verse-by-verse teaching under Senior Pastor Rodney Finch. During those eight years she participated and volunteered at multiple conferences and created a collection of poetry, "Long Talk Little Walk." Most recently she wrote the foreword for Girl, Don't Drop Your Sword by Rebecca Moran. She is reachable through her website seetarawalking.com.

CHAPTER 43

Notice: Construction In Progress Ahead

According to Luke 3:5 *"The valleys will be filled, and the mountains and hills made level. The curves will be straightened, and the rough places made smooth."*

In reading this scripture, it brought to mind a story my friend once told me about praise dancing and spiritual warfare. She told me that some places that she was invited to dance in worship were like dancing over rocks. On the contrary, she mentioned dancing other places was like floating on air. At the time she told me this I could not relate. As I reflect on her testimony, I now know it was true. The Holy Spirit brought back to my remembrance a personal experience with similar warfare and ease while praise dancing.

Several years before this an artist invited me to participate as a background vocalist on her current project. I was excited and honored that she would extend an invitation. To set the record straight, I do not claim to have a voice in caliber with anyone you probably admire and respect. However, at the time I was taking voice lessons once a week and singing regularly in a church choir. Therefore, at the very least, I expected to carry a note or two.

I arrived at the rehearsal earlier than expected, so I was able to observe everyone else as they arrived… except for one person, who was already present because they were working on their own project with the artist & their spouse. I was in the very beginning stages of knowing about the gift of discerning spirits. As the other vocalists arrived, I got a gnawing feeling that something was not right. The atmosphere was awful, perhaps akin to dancing over rocks.

Worshipping the Lord is what I love to do. I believe singing is one way he has given me to worship Him. Singing is something I have done most of my life as an activity. I was always under the impression that it was a genetic inheritance. I had family members who sang so I felt inclined to sing too. Sounds simple until it comes time for me to perform. I have been aware of, shall we call it stage fright since I was in grade school.

As I look back, I can recall a time, during a studio recording, when I was unable to release a sound out of my mouth. What is strange is that I was being coached by an accomplished professional teacher and she had full confidence in my singing abilities. So that was not the issue. Yet, when we began to sing the most awful noise was coming out of my mouth. When awful noises were not coming out of my mouth, nothing was coming out. I was breathing and projecting, but no sound came out of my mouth.

Later it was confirmed that there was a situation that manifested itself through the people who were involved in this recording. The gnawing feeling, I had that something was not right was not just a feeling, it was a fact. This insight allowed me to better understand the gift God had awakened in me to assist with intercession. I have talked about a worship dancer experiencing the feeling of dancing over rocks and myself being tortured by trying to get decent sounds to come out of my mouth while attempting to sing worship music. My friend was more talented than me in dance and also more spiritually mature than me, when it came to spiritual warfare. Therefore, when she danced you would probably not notice any trouble, she was having because of spiritual warfare taking place. As a matter of fact, the atmosphere changes because the servants of God begin to win the battle because of her worship. Now, my singing was another story at the time.

Isaiah 40:3 says, *"Listen! It's the voice of someone shouting, "Clear the way through the wilderness for the Lord! Make a straight highway through the wasteland for our God!"*

The illustration the Holy Spirit used taught me that intercession prepares the way for the LORD to enter into the lives of those who are in need of His presence. Our LORD heals, delivers, and sets free when given total access and our full surrender. Intercession makes His way secure by praying His will for hearts, minds, and territories. The presence of the LORD is ushered in by the prayers of the intercessors making straight the highway.

In times past the intercessors have prepared the way for the Spirit of God to enter. Now, intercessors are preparing the highway for the physical appearance of our God. The King of Kings will return to rule and reign in fulfillment of His Word. The intercession is the heavy equipment that uproots obstacles, agitates the ground, and pours the asphalt for the LORD's return. The instructions for the highway come straight from the Word of God therefore His will is being done on Earth as it is in heaven.

As the Son went away to prepare a place for His disciples, the intercession was preparing the earth for His return. It parallels the Jewish marriage tradition. The Bridegroom goes to prepare his home for his betrothed Bride to reside. While the bride is in the company of her family awaiting the Bridegroom to claim her as his own forever.

The LORD called me into intercession as a display of His Love by pairing our hearts, His and mine, and bringing forth His plans on the earth. The plans of the highway that the Bridegroom will use to expedite His return for His Bride. Come LORD!

About the Intercessor

Kimberly Clayton

Dr. Kimberly K. Clayton has her Christian Counseling Certificate, Community Chaplain's License, a Masters in Biblical Studies and her Honorary Doctorate in Prayer and Intercession from Ecclesia Leadership Institute that is led by Dr. Elaine Spencer (see https://ecclesialeaders.info). She enjoys receiving and completing her God-given assignments, winning souls for Jesus Christ, spending quality time with her daughter, Elise.

Dr. Kimberly is the founder and leader of "It's Praying Time," a ministry where prayer intercession and training takes place weekly. She believes in the power of prayer and intercession and is determined to help others grow in this calling.

Through "School of the Prophet" Dr. Kimberly is also an ordained and licensed minister and received her second baptism with her daughter at her side. Their mother-daughter baptism is one of her most cherished accomplishments. "School of the Prophet" is led by their fearless leader, Prophetess Renee Gordon.

CHAPTER 44

Jesus Prayed and Still Does

Jesus was a PRAYING MAN here on this earth. Jesus knew that life in this world at times can be very hard and chaotic without a solid prayer life. Jesus had no qualms about praying to God the Father. It is amazing to see how Jesus would often withdraw to secluded places to be one on one with Father God (Luke 5:16).

Jesus did not try to do his crucial ministry without help from God Almighty. He could have easily said, "I GOT THIS!" As Jesus trained his disciples, he continually pointed them to God Almighty through his actions and definitely in his prayers (John 4:34 & Mark 6:5-13). Jesus could have very well kept most of his prayers silent within himself, but the Bible clearly shows us that Jesus Christ was audible with his prayers.

Jesus showed us that great things at his level and beyond would not be possible without a solid prayer life. When the people were tired and hungry, Jesus ensured that the people could eat with just five loaves of bread and two fish to feed thousands of men, women, and children. Jesus prayed over the food (Mark 6:41) and ABBA Father blessed it and there was more than enough (when they should have ran out), they had leftovers, a miracle in itself (Mark 6:42-44). Jesus valued the POWER OF PRAYER beyond what he could get from Father God, but for what Father God could truly do through him. Jesus was not a lone ranger; he believed in teamwork, and it is evident in how he operated daily.

Jesus showed SUPERNATURAL ACCOUNTABILITY. Although he was the leader here on earth (as he trained the disciples and the masses that clung to him) he reported back to the Father for instructions, love and replenishing through his prayer life. Jesus knew that preparation comes from a lot of prayer. It is often pointed out that Jesus prepared most of his life for three amazing years of ministry!

Prayer gave Jesus strength to be committed to what he was truly put on this earth to fulfill. Jesus faced a great deal of agony in the Garden of Gethsemane. Jesus sought

Father God for another way to fulfill his ultimate purpose of coming to this earth. He needed his inner circle of disciples to hold him up in prayer; they simply just could not do so; they were too tired to keep watch with him (Matthew 26:40). Jesus' prayer life and personal relationship assured that in a very difficult moment for him, that God would make sure that he had the support and strength needed, even if an angel had to do it! (Luke 22:43)

Jesus warned his inner circle of the danger of not being able to watch and pray (keep watch) at such an intense time; that the flesh is weak, but the spirit is willing (Matthew 26:41). Let us continue to keep watch and pray, especially in the last of the last of evil days.

While on the cross, which was one of the most humiliating punishments and deaths that one could face during that time, Jesus still managed to pray for those who mocked, ridiculed, and taunted him. While here on Earth, Jesus was a man of love and forgiveness. He asked Father God to forgive them for they know not what they do according to (Luke 23:34). WOW! How many people can truly say that they ask God Almighty to forgive their MOST TREACHEROUS ENEMIES while they are hurting you? Do they really mean it from the bottom of their heart? (Matthew 6:14-15) Take a few moments and really pause, think, pray about, and actually give it a try.

Prayer was an important part of Jesus's relationship with God Almighty; the demands of ministry and his true calling had to be undergirded and sealed in powerful prayer. Jesus knew deep within that his prayer life (his personal relationship) with Father God was what was truly sustaining him, helping him to obey and stay the course that God Almighty had for him. Jesus understood that true ministry does deplete energy and virtue. Remember the lady with the issue of blood touched the hem of his garment, but her faith released virtue from Jesus that blessed her with a miraculous healing (Luke 8:46-48). JESUS UNDERSTOOD THAT PRAYER AND REST ARE THE BEST SELF-CARE TECHNIQUES (Mark 6:30-32).

The scriptures let us know, to this day, that Jesus continues in intercession as he sits on the right hand of the Father (Romans 8:34). Jesus still cares about us, and he knows very well what we are up against (John 15:17-20 & John 17:6-26). So as he prays continually, so should we as his Born-Again Disciples (1 Thessalonians 5:17). Jesus promised us that we would do GREATER WORKS (John 14:12), but we must do what Jesus did to accomplish those GREATER WORKS: PRAY, KEEP THE FAITH, TRUST GOD ALMIGHTY, OBEY FAITHFULLY AND REST.

About the Intercessor

Prophet Joshua A. De Sousa

Joshua A. De Sousa is a minister, conference speaker, youth leader, ghostwriter, and writing coach, using every opportunity possible to glorify God with his written and spoken words. He is a native of New Jersey and has been preaching the Gospel since the age of 14 years old. Joshua's online ministry presence, "De Sousa Declares Devotionals," comprises his daily social media posts, a blog, YouTube videos, and a newly launched podcast. As a writing coach, he provides prayerful support, wisdom, and strategy for hundreds through his annual online writing conference, "Supernatural Scribes." Joshua has four other books in different Christian genres. The first two from 2020 are a devotional and sermon collection entitled Dew Drops of Destiny Vol. 1: A Plethora of Prayers, Promises, and Proclamations, and a Christian superhero novel entitled The Kairos Knight Scroll I: The Remnant. The other two are a Christian writing manual called AUTHOR-ity: The Scribe Guide, and a ministry manual for preachers and Christian entrepreneurs called Multifaceted Ministry.

CHAPTER 45

Angelic Assistance
Based on Daniel 10

I am so grateful for the privilege of prayer that God has given us when He had every right to ignore us. He was gracious enough to come down as Jesus and pay the price for our sins, so that when He sees us praying, He sees His Son instead of our sin. We can now talk to God anytime and anywhere without waiting for a priest, preacher, pastor, or prophet to pray for us. That is what God is requiring of us in this season. He honors the prayers of those who pray for you, but He wants to hear you. Your voice is valuable to Him, and He is not looking for you to sound like your favorite ministry leader. He wants to remind you-you are enough as you are and are worthy of His attention. It is time to grow up and mature from the person who needs prayer and become the person who prays for everyone else.

When you look at Daniel 10, you see that God's chosen prophet was in a season of prayer and fasting because of the various crises and confusion plaguing the land he lived in. He availed himself to intercession for about three long weeks, and he was growing tired and weary from the natural sacrifices he made of sleeplessness and limited eating. Finally, an angel came through and told Daniel that God heard his prayers the first day he started petitioning Heaven. However, the angels did not deliver the answers and power Daniel needed without having to fight the darkness clouding the atmosphere around the region. Honestly, this text proves that while the angels are powerful, they are not invincible nor above restriction. When I talk about "Angelic Assistance" this message is not about the angels assisting you, but about you assisting the angels.

In order to assist the angels that are assigned like Amazon to deliver your promises from God, all you need to do is walk in authenticity, audacity, and availability. First, let us deal with authenticity. For too long, conditioning has caused us to think that the deacons, pastors, bishops, and our spirit-filled parents and grandparents are prayer experts. We feel that because of how eloquent or lengthy their prayers are, we will never reach their level of prayer or get the same attention from God as they do. God does not care about the quantity of your words; He is only concerned about the quality of the posture of your heart. Jesus instructs us in Matthew 6:5-8 to not pray as a performance so that you can impress others and appear holy and powerful. Your private prayers are important, even when all you have to give God is the tears in your eyes. Be yourself and do not compare or mimic others, for God cannot hear you if you are trying to be somebody else.

When you realize God wants your authenticity and does not need you to sound like everyone else, you can now develop the audacity needed to "come boldly to the throne of grace, that we may obtain mercy and find grace to help in time of need" as it says in Hebrews 4:16. The Lord wants you to come with confidence as if you were talking to a parent, guardian, or trusted friend, believing that He will provide you with answers and access to what you need to fulfill His plan for your life. He does not want you to be vague with your prayers because you are still walking in the fear of being disappointed. He wants you to be specific and bold enough to ask for the unusual and impossible, for it is the ultimate example of your faith. Ask Him to heal your body! Ask Him to make your name great for His glory! Ask Him to break the curse! Give God an opportunity to show you miracles of biblical proportions!

Last, you need availability to ensure that your authentic and audacious prayers receive answers and delivery. Prayer is not a one-time event, and you need to stop getting so easily discouraged when you do not see an answer after the first time you seek the Lord. Your prayers must remain consistent so that the Spirit of the Lord inside of your breath is the wind beneath the angels' wings! The enemy is going to do whatever he and his minions can to frustrate the angels assigned to you and discourage you from diving deeper into intercession. Do not give up but keep knocking on the door of Heaven through kneeling, for your rhythm of prayer shall release revival in your region! Knocking develops into authority and ownership, for you now have keys to the kingdom because you have recognition in Heaven and even hell as a force to be reckoned with!

The power of God flows through available and willing vessels, and as infinite and almighty as He is, He still needs your participation to bring forth the miracle for which you are believing. A mother can be ready to birth her child, but it is not enough for the doctors, nurses, and midwives to push from the outside. She must also push from within in order to bring forth her offspring. A butterfly also cannot expect another butterfly to dig them out of their chrysalis, but they must break themselves out, which also gives them the strength needed to fly on their own. In the same manner, the Lord and His angels are counting on your prayers, your praise, and your posture so that they can deliver your promise! He was not deaf when your prayers from several seasons ago went forth, but your angels are yet plowing through the resistance of the enemy! Keep pushing in prayer, sowing and consecration, because these things will help you push your breakthrough out of your womb!

About the Intercessor

KaSonya Miller

Hi, I am KaSonya Miller. I'm a Christian Writer, and an Inspirational Writer. I like to write about positive things, scriptures, and real-life experiences. I also like to write about prayer. As the years passed, I had a passion to connect with others in a positive way. God blessed me and I have become a Certified Christian Life Coach Professional, and a Mentor. I have a Certificate in Counseling and Therapy and Becoming a Health and Wellness Coach. I was blessed to graduate from Apostle and Prophetic Ministry Bootcamp & Prophetic Ministry and Mentoring Academy with WLMI Ministry. It did not stop there. I joined with Dr. Monique Rodgers in her book collaboration, Called To Intercede, in Volume 1. It has been such a blessing to be able to be a blessing to others, and I hope that you enjoy my chapter, I also hope to grow with you also.

CHAPTER 46

I Overcame by the Grace of God

Growing up as one of five children, I experienced and saw things that followed me into adult life. As I grew through those years, I also went through adversity. However, I kept the faith, believing things would be better. I knew there was something more in my spirit because through the adversity, God the Father, the Lord Jesus Christ, and the Holy Ghost were with me. I do not like doing wrong. When I did wrong, the conviction I felt led me to ask God for forgiveness.

God is a loving God. He will forgive you too. For example, if you have a misunderstanding with someone, quickly forgive them and love your brother and sister. Ephesians 4:32 KJV says, *"And be ye kind one to another, tenderhearted, forgiving one another, even as God for Christ's sake hath forgiven you."*

I experienced things in my life pertaining to lack, health, relationships, and understanding. Through God, and prayer, He kept me. It is vital to be obedient. All glory goes to God. I overcame by the Grace of God.

At times when I had a goal to achieve. I would pray and ask God to help me. Like when I wanted to get my Diploma in Nursing, I succeeded by the Grace of God. Prior to achieving this, I did not know how I was going to make it, but God! God has blessed me with more than I ever thought I would have. If you put God first… trust, believe, and live for Him, He will bless you too.

Genesis 28:3 KJV" And God Almighty bless thee, and make thee fruitful, and multiply thee, that thou mayest be a multitude of people."

Deuteronomy 1:11 KJV "The LORD God of your fathers make you a thousand times so many more as ye are, and bless you, as he hath promised you!"

When you turn to God, He will not fail you. You have to make up your mind and want to do better. I believe in prayer, and I believe God answers prayer. I lay aside what

I think is best for me, because I trust God and know His way is best. I know I overcame by the Grace of God.

Having experienced the hardships and breakthroughs I mentioned earlier, I know it was by the Grace of God that I made it. I had experiences in my dreams seeing Jesus, even when not so nice things were happening. Jesus would always come into my dreams. He was saving me even then. I also realize it's about being around like-minded people. When you aren't, you can be led astray. Be mindful and be in relationships where they want to see you doing better. You are supposed to love others, remember that. Also be mindful of what is not of God. God wants us to have His blessings, read Deuteronomy 11:26-27. I choose to be better because I want the blessings of God. He wants the best for my family, friends, and the people that enjoy my writings.

God will help you overcome the things you face. Keep pressing into Him in prayer and your breakthrough will come. God has blessed me to be a blessing to others. I am now an author, writer, Certified Christian Life Coach Professional, Mentor, Counselor, and I am becoming a Health and Wellness coach. All glory to God, I overcame by the grace of God.

I really did not understand relationships. The way I thought it should be never worked out. So, I asked God and wondered what I was doing wrong. Day after day I would be as nice as I possibly could to everyone. Sometimes being nice did not matter to others, which made me sad. I encountered this in my family, and even at work. I would still speak, no matter how the others reacted. When I was out shopping, I would talk to people I didn't even know. Sometimes we would talk about God, and Jesus, and people asked me to pray for them. We prayed together. It made me feel good that God was in the midst of us. I thank God for sending me to be a blessing to others. All glory goes to God.

John 15:7 KJV "If ye abide in me, and my words abide in you, ye shall ask what ye will, and it shall be done unto you."

Philippians 4:6 KJV "Be careful for nothing; but in everything by prayer and supplication with thanksgiving let your requests be made known unto God."

We never know how things will work out; we can only hope things work out well. The choices I made were not always smart. I've made mistakes being around people who weren't in my best interest. By the Grace of God, He watched over me and shielded me. You have to stay prayed up. I encouraged my children also to put God, the Lord Jesus Christ, and the Holy Ghost first. I pray that God puts His shield of protection over them and my grandchildren. Teach your children while they are young. Pray for your children and with them.

1 John 4:11 KJV "Beloved, if God so loved us, we ought also to love one another."

Deuteronomy 31:6 KJV "Be strong and of good courage, fear not, nor be afraid of them: for the LORD thy God, he it is that doth go with thee; he will not fail thee, nor forsake thee."

I thank God for all He has done for me, and for giving me more wisdom, knowledge, and understanding to be a blessing to others, and allowing me to share what I know with those that read my writings. I hope you succeed in every area of your life. I overcame by the grace of God. Look unto Him because He is your help.

About the Intercessor

Prophetess Venita Sarvis

Prophetess-Minister Venita Sarvis is a minister and one of seven founding members of Kingdom Life Ministries in Grand Rapids, MI. She is an effective, vigorous, and knowledgeable preacher and teacher of God's Word. Minister Venita is being used to pray and intercede for lost souls that are bound with life challenging issues and feelings of hopelessness and despair. She has been used to minister too many with a prophetic Word from the Lord and has received testimonies of God's healing and deliverance and His sovereign grace through her ministry. She has ministered in prayer services, and outreach ministries. She serves and feeds the homeless in the community. She believes that the power of God and continual prayers can change lives and the world.

She is a graduate of Cornerstone University where she received a BA in Business Management. She is the owner of a private catering and baking business. Minister Venita cherishes her role of being a mother to Nycole Cotto (son-in-law Mario Cotto) and is ecstatic about her role as a grandmother to her one grandson, Levi Owen.

CHAPTER 47

Called To Intercede

Called to intercede is nothing more than having a heart-to-heart conversation with God regarding the cares of life and the cares of this world. Every child of God has an opportunity to intercede. This call is vital to the souls that are lost and tender to God's heart.

Being called to intercede is operated by faith, love, trust, obedience, respect, honor, and surrendering yourself to God in prayer.

God never wanted anyone to be lost. God's love and passion for His children qualified us for the call to intercede. Your voice has the sound of a trumpet that needs to be intact throughout the world. Your voice carries weight and power. Your voice generates fear and trembling in demons. God's heart is changed when we intercede for others and situations.

The scripture that comes to mind is 2 Chronicles 7:4 ESV *"If my people, which are called by my name, shall humble themselves, and*

pray and seek my face, and turn from their wicked ways; then will I hear from heaven, and will I forgive their sin, and will I heal their land."

God's heart is to accomplish this through intercession from His people. Our voice matters to God.

About the Intercessor

Pastor Felicia Arnett

Felicia Arnett, was born and raised in Quincy, Fl. The oldest of five siblings. Raised in a small town, by mother and stepfather. The realist. My middle sister wrote music, and my youngest sister led those songs.

Intercessor, Evangelist, Pastor of New Vision Covenant Ministries. Founder of Empowering Women, Inc. Founder and owner of Caring & Loving Hands Services, LLC. Soon to have Divine Staffing Agency.

Wife, mother of 4, 2 nana babies. Before she was an entrepreneur, she worked in healthcare with many specialists. She was born and raised as a believer, and she found time serving and helping others in the community. After completing several years in corporate healthcare, she decided to take a leap of faith and go after her passion, where she shared love and freedom through the community, and people with disabilities. She's a homemaker and companion throughout the 2A region in Florida and now central Florida.

Today she is completing her first writing assignment.

CHAPTER 48

Strategy of an Intercessor

There is so much I want to write about. When I was a young teen, my parents took me to Walt Disney World. My siblings and I were very excited. I always had a passion to go see the fun activities at Walt Disney World. While visiting that amusement park, there was so much to do and see. I ran into a section there where they played music and a selective show about every 45 minutes. There seems to be anxiety and nervousness going on all around me. I was feeling anxious and lightheaded. At that moment, I knew something wasn't quite right. I touched my stomach and prayed to the Father, "Have mercy upon me."

I felt at an early age the need to pray for something. I felt the need to pray for myself. As intercessors, we have that drive to pray for ourselves as well to the heavenly father. There is no such thing as short or long prayer. You don't have to always get on your knees to pray. You can pray while working, cooking, and driving.

An intercessor must first build a relationship with the heavenly father. An intercessor connects with the Holy Spirit. Build yourself in GOD. Reading and studying the word of GOD is another way to build yourself up. As an Intercessor you must make sacrifices and submit as a willing vessel. As an intercessor, often you may feel you cannot pray and don't feel the need to pray. 1Thessalonians 5:17 "Pray continually". As an intercessor, you should always pray. Pray when you are up, pray when you are down. Pray when you are feeling well, pray when you are not feeling well.

Living the life of an intercessor calls you to make sacrifices. We, as believers, need to have our lives filled with extreme consecration and intense intercession. Yet, as we read stories of spiritual warfare in the Bible, we humans have an important part to play. We also learn that "prayer of a person living right with GOD is something powerful to be reckoned with," (James 5:16). A consecrated Christian given to consistent intercession is more powerful than any make-believe Jedi using the make-believe force.

And now is the time we Christians are being called into battle by JESUS, our commander.

Right now, I know in my mind that JESUS, our commander, is calling all Christians to fervent prayer. I know in my mind there are spiritual forces in spiritual defiance of what GOD has promised in our time and space in this season. I know our prayers can change the momentum of the current forces leading us into self-centeredness and self-destruction, into additional forces that bring humility and godly renewal to our city.

So, let's shake off the lethargy, awaken from our spiritual stupor, and boldly enter the throne of GOD on behalf of our children, spouses, families, city, church, and households. Prayer through intercession is so powerful. Intercession changes the very heartbeat of GOD. INTERCESSION equips you and prepares you for what is coming next.

No matter what comes your way or what you face, you can conquer anything through prayer and intercession. So, let us wake up, arise and go forth, intercessors, like an eagle. Let's keep soaring higher and higher.

Do not take your INTERCESSION lightly.

GOD has more for you to do through INTERCESSION.

About the Intercessor

Pastor Angela Walker

Pastor Angela committed her life to Christ in 1984. She was saved under the preaching and teaching of Apostle R. L. Mitchell of the Old Landmark Church in Chicago, IL. Three days after God saved her, she was filled with the gift of the Holy Ghost. She was called by God in 1989 as a Messenger of Truth and commissioned to go forth in boldness teaching and preaching His word. God has anointed her to write and sing songs of Worship and Praise. Her first CD entitled, "God Will Never Change, has blessed many. She is defined as a True Worshipper and Intercessor. Gifted with many talents by God, she served as Praise & Worship Leader, Choir Director, Soloist, Evangelist, Conference Speaker and Coordinator as well as Emcee, TV, and Radio Announcer. She published her first book in 2015 entitled, "Overcoming the Limits, You Are Unstoppable."

Pastor Angela was a part of a global Evangelistic Mission Team under the leadership of Former COGIC Mission President, Bishop Carlis Moody. They traveled to the devastated areas of Haiti July 2010 after the 7.0 earthquake to help bring healing to the land. In 2011, they travelled to Guyana, South America to minister to the needs of His people. Souls were saved, demons cast out, blinded eyes opened, and lives forever changed including her own.

Pastor Angela was consecrated as Pastor in 2013 under Apostle R. L. Johnson, of the Church of God in Christ of Americas. She relocated to Nashville, TN in 2013 and became the Lead Servant of Triumphant Life Church (TLC) in LaVergne, TN. In 2015, she travelled to Cameroon Africa to partner with a team of Spiritual and Business Professional Leaders from around the world to conduct seminars, workshops and services empowering the community. She has been summoned by God to call souls around the world to repentance and righteousness by hearing of His anointed word and spreading the love of Jesus. She inspires others through social media engagement and weekly teaches Bible Study to a group of believers in Pakistan who are sold out for Jesus. Angela yields to God's voice and His timing to make full proof of her ministry.

Pastor Angela currently resides in Calera, AL. She is the mother of three sons, the grandmother of two grandsons and one granddaughter.

CHAPTER 49

The Place of Preparation

When I think of a true Warrior, I think of King David. David was anointed by God for the deliverance of His people, but his calling was not without opposition. Highly anointed, he was pressured by the enemy and his very life threatened. He was pursued to the point that he hid in a cave called Adullam. Adullam in Greek means "a hiding place, retreat or refuge." The word of God in Psalm 91:1 declares, *"He that dwelleth in the secret place of the Most High shall abide under the shadow of the Almighty."*

When the enemy has you in a corner, he thinks that he has the advantage, but what he fails to realize is that this is the place God wants us to be and it allows Him the opportunity to show Himself strong and mighty on our behalf. This pushes us into a posture of prayer causing us to cry out to the God who can do exceedingly abundantly above all that we ask or think according to the power that works in and through us (Ephesians 3:20).

Adullam was the place where God called David to be secluded, secure and sanctified. God separates him that is godly for Himself (Psalm 4:3). There is a reason for every relationship that has ended abruptly. There is a reason you feel alone and there is no one that you can rely on. Initially, it was fear that drove David into this place, but faith brought him out. He did not come out the same way he went in. While in this place, the drawing anointing that was upon David's life caused others to be pulled into the place of hiding where they too could be revived, refreshed, restored, and pushed to another dimension to combat the enemy. When it seems that the enemy is doing his worst, God is at work to bring out the best because He has plans to prosper us and not harm us. He does not chasten us to see how much we can bear, but He brings us to the threshing floor to purge us and cause the anointing to flow through us as vessels of honor.

In this hiding place, David was able to minister and pray for others as he needed strength and encouragement himself. What you make happen for others, God will make happen for you. When you forget about your heaviness and carry the burdens of others in prayer before the throne of God, there will be a release in the spirit on your behalf. These men were broken, discouraged, in depth and felt there was nothing left. While in the secret place, they had a God encounter. They learned the secret of stealing away and emptying out before Him (Psalm 62:8). The enemy comes not but to steal, to kill, and destroy. Jesus said, but I am come that you may have life more abundantly (John 10:10). The abundant life comes when we realize we have power with God. We have the power within us to decree and declare as we believe God to move on our behalf as we speak in faith over every situation, circumstance, and obstacle that we face. We trust in the Sovereignty of who God is and what He said His word will accomplish when released into the atmosphere.

We take authority and our rightful positions as sons of God who have been called to rule over the powers that operate in the earth realm. God has given us power to loose and to bind. *"Verily I say unto you, Whatsoever ye shall bind on earth shall be bound in the heaven; and whatsoever ye shall loose on earth shall be loosed in heaven"* Matthew 18:18. We have the power to restrict or release by the word of God. If we choose to do nothing, we give the enemy permission to do what he deems appropriate. But when true warriors take their position as watchmen on the wall, we see the enemy afar off and sound the alarm declaring war against the enemy of our souls. We command him hitherto shalt thou come, but not further (Job 38:11). We invite the presence of God to overtake and overthrow the plans of the enemy. We invoke His presence and summon the angels that have been assigned to war on our behalf to do battle in the spirit realm. It is not by power, nor by might, but by the spirit of the Almighty God that Satan is put to flight because he is not welcomed. He is a trespasser and the opposer of all that is righteous. He comes to wear out the patience of the Saints but let us not become weary in our well doing for in do season, we shall reap if we faint not (Galatians 6:9).

The men that followed David, began to do war in secret and when they ascended from the cave, they were a force to be reckoned with. They were equipped and empowered to withstand every enemy that came their way by the power of God. They did not retreat even when it seemed they were outnumbered, recognizing that if God be for us, no one is able to stand against us. They were men that were apt to battle. As we submerge in prayer, while consecrating ourselves before the Lord, God is covering us with the covering of heaven that demons will tremble as they did when Jesus showed up. Satan will recognize you when you are intentional about your seek and search after God. The weapons of our warfare are not carnal but mighty through God to the pulling down of strong holds and casting down vain imaginations and every high thing that exalts itself against the knowledge of God (2 Corinthians 10:4).

It is time for the true warriors to take their place in secret so God can launch you forward to do damage against the Kingdom of Darkness.

About the Intercessor

Dr. Patricia Rogers

I am Dr. Patricia Rogers, Visibility Strategist & CEO of Unity In Service, Inc. "Where People Need People." Since obtaining my business name "Unity In Service, Inc., in 2012, I was still employed in corporate America. Coming up on my retirement of 29 years in law enforcement, I retired as a corrections lieutenant in 2016.

I realized that to live my life on my terms, using my gifts and talents to impact the lives of others was essential to enjoying my retirement and becoming a successful entrepreneur.

Yes, it is evident that preparation was the key to my success as an entrepreneur, so I invested in coaches who were influencers in the entrepreneur space. Those individuals were successful, and they had what I wanted.

What I Wanted:

I desired to be a successful entrepreneur once I was retired so that I did not have to work for anyone else in life.

Today, I have positioned myself as an International Best-Selling Author| Business Coach Virtual Event Host| International Public Speaker. My most recent achievement is the "Honorary Doctor of Humanity Award," and the doors continue to open.

According to Psalms 37:4 *"Delight yourself in the Lord, and He will give you the desires of thine heart."* What I will add to that passage is, "if we do the work, the increase has to come."

Politics In the Workplace:

The politics in the workplace made my life difficult at times. When you stand up for your rights, it can get worse before it gets better. You become a target!

When you challenge the system for violating your employee rights, administrative personnel abuse their authority and retaliate against you.

One may wonder, how do you survive ridicule and disparate treatment? God chooses you to be a beacon of light so that others who are watching will see the miraculous hand of God upon your life. You will be tried!

1 Peter 1:7 states, *"That the trial of your faith, being much more precious than of gold that perisheth, though it be tried with fire, might be found unto praise and honor and glory at the appearing of Jesus Christ."*

Challenges are a part of your conditioning, and to benefit from the challenges, you must practice patience and have a strong belief in God, that those things are working out for your good.

CHAPTER 50

What's For You is Yours: God's Promises are True

Called to Serve:

My mother of eight children raised us in the church, and God had a calling on my life from the beginning, and every challenge that I had in the workplace would work out in my favor. The department arbitrarily passed over me for promotions. I faced false allegations at times and experienced feelings of inadequacy. This would cause me to ask myself, why am I here? People's negative behaviors are designed to stop you from reaching your highest potential. Still, they did not know that my life was hidden in Christ Jesus, and whatever I ask in His name, believing, will happen. I kept my eyes on God, and I knew that His Word was true. John 15:16 says, "Ye have not chosen me, but I have chosen you, and ordained you, that ye should go and bring forth fruit, and that your fruit should remain; that whatsoever you shall ask of the Father in my name, he may give it you."

The Best is Yet to Come:

I also knew who I was and where I was going. Every challenge was guaranteed to set me up for something great! Today, I am an entrepreneur, and I host virtual events for entrepreneurs to speak to enlarge their audience. I coach entrepreneurs on making an impact when they show up on social media. I am living my wildest dreams, and I thank God for allowing me to enjoy the fruit of my labor! I knew that God had orchestrated my role as a leader. I also knew that people were watching to see how I would face each challenge. However, they did NOT know that there was a power inside me that was much greater than any challenge they threw my way! God created you for His purpose. When you have a personal relationship with the Divine, you can overcome every opposition.

Keeping Your Vision in View:

The relationship you have with God holds Him accountable to intercede on your behalf to the Father. Challenges set you up for opportunities that condition and shape you for the next chapter in your life. You were handpicked and called to serve, and the challenges are by divine purpose. The only requirement is to keep believing and interceding and do the work as if your request has already come to fruition. For me, I kept my eyes on the prize, which was my retirement! God planted me in my place of employment, and only God could take me out! Quitting is never an option! I stood fast on the promises of God, and before I knew it, I received and earned various promotions. I was given various accolades during my tenure, and my pension is in the mail every month as long as I live. These are only a few of the rewards for persevering. Having a colossal retirement celebration that included horses and a carriage, I arrived at my retirement dinner as the queen I had become. Many families and friends were there to celebrate my achievement, and it was a fantastic affair.

What is the Point?

If you have a burning desire to achieve your goal, do not let anyone stand in your way! If you are still working toward a specific goal, keep your eyes on the prize, stay focused on your "Why," and know that a moving target is hard to hit! Keep walking into your destiny! You were born to win! The bricks that are thrown at you are only stepping stones. You get to write the closing chapter of your journey.

Connect with Dr. Patricia Rogers @ PatRogers360.com

About the Intercessor

Minister Latoshi Russell-McMorris

My name is Latoshi (Russell) McMorris born and raised in Dowagiac, Michigan, however my roots are from Mississippi. Growing up I always knew I was different and called to do great things. During my time in school, I was a very high achiever in sports and academics from being on honor roll, to the dean's list, then followed by collegiate honors. In 2013, I obtained my associates degree in business management and plan to return.

In 2009, I was called in the office of the Evangelist coupled with prophetic grace. I currently serve at my church as a minister, praise, and worship leader, and I also operate in the gifts of hospitality. I love God, I love my husband and our dog Lydia. In my free time I enjoy helping others, traveling, levels of relaxation, and family time.

CHAPTER 51

The Encounter

As a child, I was always called on to help others, which I love, by the way. When a child is young, they desire to be just that... a child. Not an adult before their time. I had so many overwhelming responsibilities. God showed himself to me many times growing up as a child, and as a young adult. There is one experience that sticks out to me more than anything else. I called it my first encounter with God. I took college prep classes during high school, but I almost dropped out by the 10th Grade from reaching an all-time low. I could not wake up for class and had to speak to the guidance counselor to see if I could start school later. Even with rescheduled classes, I still kept failing. Dressing nice did not matter to me anymore, arriving at school in jogging pants and a shirt tied to the side and my hair in a ponytail. I failed two classes that year and took nine just to graduate on time. I took a "zero" hour, coming to school an hour earlier than regular class time, my regular 6-hour classes throughout the day, and two-night classes.

I graduated in June of 1996 and began college in September of the same year. However, I had difficulty breathing, irregular heartbeats, and constant sweating in class by November. At first, I assumed they were heart attacks. The last time I was in class, I could feel the "episode" about to happen. Immediately, I grabbed my things and ran out of the class. As I drove to the hospital, I had not noticed that my heartbeat was back to normal. Fear consumed me as I checked in, and they diagnosed me with panic attacks. I was nineteen and had never even heard of them. The panic attacks became more frequent, and I found myself running to either the ER or to my doctor's office weekly. On my last visit to see my doctor, she referred me to a behavior health center where I was put on Xanax and Paxil. She eventually released me as her patient, stating what I was dealing with was out of her source of education. I was left alone to deal with what my body was experiencing as reality.